HELP! MY CHILD STOPPED EATING MEAT!

HELP! MY CHILD STOPPED EATING MEAT!

An A–Z Guide to Surviving a Conflict in Diets

CAROL J. ADAMS

with nutritional information by
Virginia Messina, M.P.H., R.D.

continuum
NEW YORK · LONDON

2004

The Continuum International Publishing Group Inc
15 East 26 Street, New York, NY 10010

The Continuum International Publishing Group Ltd
The Tower Building, 11 York Road, London SE17NX

Printed in the United States of America

Library of Congress Cataloging-in-Publication Data
Adams, Carol J.
    Help! my child stopped eating meat! : an A–Z guide to surviving a
conflict in diets / Carol J. Adams, with nutritional information by
Virginia Messina, M.P.H., R.D.
        p.   cm.
    ISBN 0-8264-1583-0 (pbk. : alk. paper)
    1. Vegetarian children.   2. Vegetarianism—Social aspects.   3. Child
development.   I. Title.
RJ206.A326   2004
613.2'62—dc22

                                                        2003021429

For Pat Davis and Patti Breitman—
This book's alpha and omega:
you know how to help children and books
grow and flourish;
you know how to nurture change.

Contents

Topical Chapter Listing

1. FAMILY AND EMOTIONAL ISSUES

Abundance/Scarcity • Acceptance • Accessibility • Accusation • Affection • Anger • Antiestablishment • Arguments • Attention • Authority • Benefits • Blame • Change • Communication • Community • Compassion • Conflict • Control • Conversations • Cruelty • Cult • Door Swings off the Hinges • Eating Together Ground Rules • Embarrassment • Emotions/Feelings • Engagement • Explanations • Fads • Failure • Fears • Gender Issues • Grandparents • "Grow Up" • "Hands Off" as Much as Possible • Hugs • Humor • "I'm Not Going to Fix Anything Extra!" • Impatience • "In Your Face" Veg*nism • "It's the American Thing" • "It's the End of the World" • Listening • Love • Midlife Crisis • Motivation • "My Dad . . . , My Mom . . ." • Negotiation • Neighbors, Friends, and Relatives • Nomad Year • Peer Issues • "Pick Out the Meat" • Power • Powerlessness • Rejection • Resentment • Respect • Responsibility • Responsibility Versus Self-interest • Scapegoating • Self-esteem • Shaming Techniques • Spousal/Partner Tension • Stages of Growth • Starvation • Teasing • Thanksgiving • Third-Person Communication • Time-out • Trust/Mistrust • Ultimatums • Undermining • What Do You Think? • Why? • Will • Worry

2. PRACTICAL ISSUES

Bar or Bat Mitzvahs • Birthdays • Books • Breakfast Possibilities • Candles • Celebrations • Chocolate • Chores • Colleges/Universities • Comfort Foods • Convenience Foods • Cookbooks • Cooking •

Couscous with Cinnamon and Raisins • Biscuits and gravy • Soy "butter"milk Skillet Corn Bread

Steddas and Sauces

Egg Substitute for Baked Goods • Tofu "Feta Cheese" • Tofu "Ricotta" • Tofu Ranch Dressing • Caesar Salad Dressing • Orange Tahini Sauce • Nacho Sauce • Tofu "Cottage Cheese" • Tofu Sour Cream

Sandwiches and Other Lunch Possibilities

Instant Pizzas • Basic Sandwiches • Hummus • Mock Tuna • Veggie Burger Wrap • Black Bean Wrap • Tofu Sandwich Spread • Hot Tofu Sandwich • Baked Tofu • Glazed Tofu • Tofu Fajitas • Super Nachos

Soups and Chili

Pumpkin Soup • Corn Chowder • Cream of Cauliflower Soup • Chili non Carne

Main Dishes

Mushroom Stroganoff • Comforting Pot Pie • Squash Ribbon Sauté • Linguine with Olives, Tomatoes, and Fresh Herbs • Pad Thai • Millet Croquettes • Sloppy "Janes" • Shish Kebobs • Tofu Tacos • Easy Baked Beans • Pilaf with Carrots and Raisins • Quinoa, Corn, and Potatoes • Orzo Pilaf • Stuffed Manicotti • Stuffed Acorn Squash

Veggies and Salads

Roasted Red Pepper • Lentil Salad • Greek Salad • Autumn Wheat Berry Salad • Ensalada de Frijoles • Broccoli and "Bacon" Salad • Crunchy Onion Rings • Crunchy Green Beans • Kale with Cinnamon • Scalloped Potatoes • Creamed Greens

Desserts

Chocolate-chip Cake • Mile-high Carob or Chocolate Layer Cake • Garden-Kissed Snack Cake • Banana Cake with Tofu Cream

Frosting • Peanut Butter Cookies • Maple Almond Pudding •
Ginger Peachy Bread Pudding • Cheeseque Cake from Buffalo •
Pumpkin Cream Pie

Introduction

So your child has become a vegetarian or a vegan and your life as a parent has just gotten more complicated, more challenging, perhaps more interesting, and at times worrisome if not frustrating. You love your child and want the best for your child. How does this dietary change fit into your desires for him or her?

You may be frightened by your child's desire to eliminate from the diet red meat, chicken, and fish (and perhaps milk, eggs, and cheese as well). Will your child grow and thrive on this new diet? Protein, calcium, iron, vitamins, minerals—you may have guaranteed your child's nutritional needs through serving meat and dairy products. Suddenly, the many ways you insured your child was growing up healthily are rejected.

You may be concerned that your child will die because of a seemingly restricted diet. First, let me assure you—your child can be perfectly healthy on a vegetarian or a vegan diet. Vegetarian and vegan children will reach the right height and weight for their age group. In fact, your child may now be adhering more closely to the current dietary guidelines that encourage five to nine helpings of vegetables and fruits a day. Additionally, she may now have her own motivations to ensure her protein, calcium, iron, vitamin, and mineral needs are being met. She has to show you she can survive and thrive through this new way of eating.

Nutritional concerns, while a major worry for any parent, are not the only issues that are raised as your child rejects meat. Simultaneously a whole new arena for family confrontations has opened up. Parent-child relationships, often strained by the child's journey toward and through adolescence, may become absolutely and wrenchingly broken by this rejection. Your child may ask you to read books or may bring a spotlight on what your family may continue to eat. New frustrations enter your relationship, tense dinnertime conversations erupt, and a feeling arises that the parent-child relationship has gotten (even more) contentious than it was. You are hurt that your child is accusing you of causing animals to suffer or of causing the environmental crisis. You may have begun to wonder if your child hates you or fear that some fanatical group has brainwashed your child. What's next? Will he join a cult?

People become vegetarians for a variety of reasons. In this book, I have assumed your young person has become a vegetarian for health, environmental, or ethical reasons. But people also become vegetarians for religious reasons (some religions, such as Seventh-Day Adventism, advocate vegetarianism). Others become vegetarian for spiritual reasons; they feel a sense of interconnectedness with the world and determine to do the least harm possible. *Ahimsā,* or nonharming, is a principle of yoga, and may be something your young person has learned about and wishes to enact. Some people become vegetarians because of an aesthetic objection to meat eating; the idea of eating dead animals simply is unappetizing. Often, someone may become a vegetarian for one reason, but as she continues in vegetarianism, the other reasons become equally compelling. While aspects of vegetarianism may seem "cultlike," especially the concern with the choice and preparation of food, vegetarianism, per se, is not a cult.

Some kids chose to be vegetarians; some kids chose to be vegans. A vegan is a person who does not consume or use any animal products. Thus, besides objecting to the killing of animals, vegans object to the use of animals to produce food, for instance, using cows to produce milk, or chickens to produce eggs, or bees, honey. Someone who does not consume any animal products might also be called a plant-based or strict vegetarian. A vegan, besides not eating any animal products, will not wear them (i.e., leather, wool, or silk), or use products that contain animals such as soaps, shampoos, candles, etc.

You might have been open to vegetarianism but feel that veganism is going too far. Generally, the motivation for veganism is compassion for living beings. The animal rights movement has provided information about the fate of animals in animal agriculture. Because of activists' tables at concerts and other venues for youth, many young people encounter this information and feel horrified to discover they support a system that treats living beings in ways that seem very cruel.

Because your relationship with your child is experiencing new stresses, you aren't just worried about the impact of her change of diet on her friendships, her health, her future. You may feel angry and ask, "What right does she have to judge me?" You may feel frantic: "I don't know anything about vegetarianism and I don't have any time to learn!" You worry "What will I feed her?" You may feel rejected because food that symbolized loving and caring in the family, perhaps for generations (whether it is Jell-O salad for sick stomachs or turkey for Thanksgiving), is being rejected.

Everywhere you turn you encounter a new issue associated with this dietary change. This is time-consuming if not exhausting and painful! And all because you love your child so much and truly do want the best for her that you are willing to hang in there with her as she explores this new way of eating.

Let me help to make this matter less time-consuming, less exhausting, and hopefully less frustrating for you. I am the author of a book that has been very important to many young vegetarians. This has given me an entrée to their experiences. They invite me to speak at their colleges—or even, sometimes, their high schools. I have met hundreds of vegetarian and vegan children who once lived under the same roof with concerned and loving parents like you. I meet kids like yours who have become young adults—and I am impressed. They are bright, compassionate, involved with the changing world, and they are vegetarians.

You are concerned about your relationship to your vegetarian child. Perhaps it helps to know that your vegetarian child is concerned about his relationship to you. If your child is like the many young people I have met, I can safely predict that your child wants your acceptance: "I don't drink. I don't hang out with a bad crowd. I'm doing something humane. Why can't my parents praise me for this instead of criticizing me?" Your child wants you not to belittle vegetarianism ("Tell my parents, 'It's not a phase'"); nor to fear it ("Tell my parents it's not going to lead to me joining a cult"). Your child wants you to worry less; no, she isn't going to die ("Tell my parents, 'There are many people who never eat meat and they haven't died as a result'"). Your child wants you to see it as a positive choice ("Tell my parents, 'You didn't do anything wrong to make me take this turn. In fact, it's to your credit'"). Finally, your child wants you to know that he can be healthy ("Tell my parents to stop worrying! I can get all the nutrients and vitamins I need").

I have also talked with numerous parents of vegetarians. They have trusted me with stories of the complicated relationships that prevail in homes where different food choices often cause conflict. I have heard encouraging stories and discouraging stories. I have distilled what I have heard and what I have learned and, with the expert nutritional help of Virginia Messina, constructed a book that I believe addresses your specific concerns.

This book offers suggestions and helpful information so that you can continue to do what you have been trying to do all along—be a supportive parent. You don't need to change your diet. But you do need to continue to grow as a parent. I say that as a parent who herself is always being challenged to grow. Like you, I love my kids deeply, overwhelmingly. I love my kids yet I have still done things that confound me in retrospect, that reveal to me a stubborn refusal to grow or even to understand. I keep a journal and encounter the angry, frustrated parent as well as the loving, caring parent in its pages. I offer to you the insights of a parent but also of someone who, at times, teaches a course in pastoral care, and has specialized in writing and counseling about broken relationships. I think about relationships a great deal and believe that communication and acceptance form a strong foundation for healthy relationships.

You will want to know that I've made a decision to be a vegan. The death of my pony in a hunting accident when I was twenty-two prompted my vegetarianism. Thinking about dead bodies, I decided I did not want to eat animals. Later, when I learned about the treatment of cows and hens, I decided to forego milk and eggs. Because of my veganism, I can think my way into what may be happening with your kids in their relationship with you. I used to feel, as a new vegetarian, what your child may now be feeling—a combination of anger with meat eating coupled with hopefulness. I used to believe that meat eaters would change once they heard about what was happening with animals and the environment. Your child may believe this and make efforts to change you. But I am not trying to convert you! I only want to give you the opportunity to experience your child's passion for vegetarianism as a positive aspect of her growth and to have the tools to help her with her anger, frustration, and optimism.

A vegetarian or vegan child in a meat-eating family can be inconvenient. That's nothing new. Children are often inconvenient! The great thing about parenting is the opportunity to discover that their growth is happening on the other side of our inconvenience. To encounter their lives and their interests we have to see beyond our inconvenience. We have to recognize that what we may label "inconvenience" is actually a sense of rejection, a sense that we cannot understand what is happening in our children's lives, a sense of frustration as a gap opens up between who we thought they were and who they actually are. In a profound way, this feeling of "inconvenience" in our lives offers a way "in" to our kids' lives. When we see beyond our inconvenience we experience, truly, who our children are and who they are becoming.

Since I am proposing that you trust my insights into *your* family dynamics, I wish to share a story from *my* family dynamics. I have experienced what it is like to be in a family when life-changing events happen in a child's life. No, the issue in our family wasn't veganism or vegetarianism, yet the dynamics were similar. I want you to know that during a life-changing time in my son's life, I experienced conflict, frustration, and impatience. His life was lived in the midst of those experiences, and because I was experiencing these emotions, I could not completely recognize just how deeply life-changing his experiences were.

As a writer, I discovered that rising at five A.M. and writing for two hours before the rest of the household awoke was extremely productive. I wrote two books that way during my older son's sophomore year in high school. This early morning time seemed to provide me with a deeper place to draw upon in my writing. I cherished that time but suspended the schedule during summer vacation, knowing I would reestablish it once school began.

As my son's junior year in high school began, I again returned to this intensely fulfilling writing schedule. Then something happened that brought about a change, a change I fought, a change I wrestled with, a change I found so frustrating. Yes, a change that inconvenienced me. It took me a year and a half to truly learn what was on the other side of that inconvenience.

One night, returning from a college information session, we discovered that a neighbor's cat had attacked our two bunnies. One was dead and the other was gravely injured. By the next morning, the other one was dead and we buried both of them before school. My older son, Douglas, felt a great deal of regret that with his busy schedule he had not spent as much time with these special bunnies as he had hoped. Going to school that day he made a pledge to himself that he would seize every opportunity that came his way; no more regrets for missed opportunities. And then, that day, out of the blue, he was asked to join band.

They had lost someone who played the vibraphone and needed someone with keyboard skills. Heeding his promise to himself, he leapt into the band position—and never looked back.

High school band in Texas is not an extracurricular activity; it is a way of life. And so it was on the very next Monday that my way of life, my early-morning writing life, came to an end. Now Douglas had to be at school by seven A.M.—a magnet school that was fifteen minutes from our house by car. Now he had to get up much earlier—and he did not awaken easily. Now my early writing time was interrupted.

My time for writing could not survive the frustration of this interruption, including a thirty-minute round-trip drive to his school, only to return and do it in another direction for his sixth-grade brother who was in a different magnet school in Dallas.

Now he had truly begun to disappear: band in the morning, band after school, band at football games, band parties. Yes, we supported him; we went to home games; we attended concerts. But we experienced band differently. While marching band to me had military overtones, marching band to Doug gave him peers who, like him, loved to make music.

I knew Doug loved band. But I couldn't handle the frustration of losing my two-hour writing time. I stopped trying to balance his schedule with mine. Mine would have to wait until he went to college.

Though he came late to the band experience, he made up for it quickly and with enthusiasm. He studied drumming and tried out for the drum line. He became a member of the leadership team. It was perfectly clear that he loved band, that he couldn't get enough of it. By his senior year, band was all-important. I *tried* to be supportive. I tried to find ways so that his schedule gave me something rather than taking something away. I began to walk in the nearby park early in the morning after dropping him off. I could hear the band playing, and I would tell myself, "A year from now it will be all different."

Then I would hurry home to take my other child, Ben, to school.

But I was, as all parents at times may be, frustrated and impatient with all the new demands my son's commitment had created. Sometimes I was furious with band when yet another family tradition had to be altered or curtailed because of it.

Again, I knew he loved it. I knew he was thriving. But I also mourned for what it had taken away. At other times, low-level frustration characterized my relationship to the *idea* of band. I mastered the art of complaining.

Then, at the end of his senior year, came the band banquet. Doug was one of four students selected by the band director to give a senior farewell. As he spoke about the band and his three band teachers and what they had taught him about making music and working as a team, many of us were deeply moved. But only I had to confront a truth that was deeply painful, too: his living, his *thriving*, had been happening where I had experienced frustration and inconvenience. As I listened to him, I realized that band had touched him so much more deeply than I had been able to appreciate. His life was there. I had not been equipped to notice this.

When Doug, along with the drum major, was voted an outstanding band student by his peers, I had to confront something else as well. His absolute love of band had made him able to be present to his peers. They knew a different Doug than I had known, and they loved and appreciated this Doug. And that is when I realized: *on the other side of my inconvenience, he was leading a deeply rewarding, joyful life.* I could not begin to understand it fully because I kept interpreting it from my viewpoint—what it had taken away. Finally, I heard eloquently from his perspective what it had given him. I was ashamed of myself for my selfishness. How much growing had been going on and I had not been equipped to notice!

I get to experience young vegetarians the way the band students experienced my son—in an atmosphere of acceptance where they are doing something they love and sharing it with others. It is such a privilege.

Perhaps I am hard on myself. I could never "know" the Doug that his peers or teachers knew. Moreover, I had never been absolutely opposed to band. But support can be uneven, frustration can often win the day, and working out day-to-day relationships (with all their attendant frustrations) is the major work of parenting. Our children are often changing in ways we cannot register. They need to change. They are becoming adults.

Believe me, when I address the issue of tension with your kids because their interests are different from yours, I speak from experience. When I describe how the "door swings off the hinges" or what the costs are of feeling what we label "inconvenience," I speak as someone who has experienced these tensions—and then had the opportunity to reflect on them.

If I can give you the opportunity to appreciate your child's *experience*, your child's *meaningful* choices, as he or she is undergoing them, then perhaps you will not have to encounter that overwhelming "band banquet" moment. You'll be able to experience the joy and growth along with your child as his or her life as a vegetarian unfolds.

Loving our children asks so much of us. The fact is it asks more than we ever anticipated. But, luckily for us, we somehow have the capacity as parents to give them more than we thought we had to give.

There is a *life* in a decision to be a vegetarian. Like band, it isn't a decision that is harmful to others but an expression of good intentions and high ideals.

The young vegetarians and vegans I have met all around the country have been smart, caring, involved, part of loving communities, appreciative of their families, interested in ideas, generous in thinking about issues, and good cooks, too! You probably have a young vegetarian and vegan living in your home just like this. But because that child is *your* child, the normal stresses of family life and parenting may prevent you from experiencing the wonderful young person your vegetarian child is becoming.

One true test of parenting is the willingness to find ways to be a parent when your child is choosing to do something that you would not do and that you cannot comprehend doing. As long as the child's choice is not unethical, illegal, or a cause of harm to herself or others then your challenge is to be able to meet her there—or if not, at least to allow her the latitude of exploration.

Choose your battles with your child. Ask yourself, Why is vegetarianism/veganism an actual or potential battleground? After all, the choice not to eat animals demonstrates aspects of growth toward adulthood that you want your child to exhibit: independence, thoughtfulness, and engagement.

As parents we cannot anticipate what will be required of us. Just when we think some sort of balance has been achieved between our interests and our child's interests, be assured something will occur that will throw off that balance. Sometimes we can't see how incredibly important and rich an experience is for our child because we are experiencing it in its guise as disruptions and demands upon us. We cannot see the positive for them because we are focused on its negative impact on our lives. It is no fun to feel constantly frustrated with your child. I learned that when my child is growing and making choices that are rich and important to him, I have to stop holding onto "my" way and find a way to examine what makes the conflict so painful.

We don't go into parenthood agreeing to support our children until it becomes inconvenient, frustrating, infuriating, or painful. Whatever the changes that prompt our feelings, we have to learn to change our belief that *we* know what is right for them better than they do. If we don't, we will be swallowed by bitterness. If we are attentive, we may be offered glimpses of the meaning of those things in their lives that have frustrated us in ours. As they stretch themselves, we find that we have stretched, too.

The process of rearing a child is a process of learning to trust that child. Our trust is compromised by our anxiety: *Can* he make the right decision? *Is* she making the right decision? Your concerns about vegetarianism may arise from the issues that accompany the process of trusting someone with decision making: Is he able to consider competing information, analyze it, and come to a decision? Are we able to let our children follow the process or do we have a need to control their decision making?

Ceding control to a child is hard; we become accustomed to many ways of being controlling. But parenting and controlling are not the same thing. Ask yourself: Do they have the information needed to make the decision? If not, how can you help them get the information? What information do you think is necessary? Do *we* have the information to be comfortable with the idea that *they* have the needed information to make a decision independent of us?

I know you are busy—after all you are rearing children. Because you are busy, I have structured this book to provide you with the information to trust your child's decision-making process or to help her or him acquire the information necessary for making such decisions. Like a dictionary, this book offers the information in easily accessible ways. Chapters on the basic issues that arise for familes, from the practical to the emotional, provide an organizational theme to the information within them. Within each chapter, alphabetical entries provide quick answers to your concerns. Cross-references are provided as well as a topical-chapter listing (pp. 9–12). Some of the entries may not apply to your situation; through their titles, you should be able to identify which ones apply and which ones don't and skip over the ones that don't. For ease of reading and because these suggestions apply both for vegan children and vegetarian children, I use a shorthand in referring to vegetarianism and veganism: "veg*nism."

My goal is to help you place veg*nism within the ordinary tensions we parents experience as our children grow up, rather than regarding it as an extraordinary and therefore unacceptable decision. I hope this book helps you to continue to enjoy your child's growth toward adulthood.

Your child is an optimist. He not only believes in change, he is living proof of change! Who can blame him for believing that if he finds the right argument, you will join him in giving up meat (and perhaps also dairy and eggs)? Don't let his optimism frustrate you—let it be a sign of youthful hopefulness.

Will vegetarianism or veganism continue in their lives when they reach the full blossoming of adulthood? Let your child decide for herself. By respecting your child as she or he explores veg*nism, you model how one respects another despite a difference of opinion. That is a great gift.

P.S. Thanks.

I was in the car with some college students. One young woman described how her mother had told her when she was fourteen, "You can't be a vegetarian unless you get information." She was so grateful for that response! She researched and learned to cook and showed her mother just how well she could live as a vegan. Now, as we drove to a bookstore, she was not just an experienced cook but an accomplished professional chef. At the bookstore, she picked out a Mother's Day card for her mother. It read, "Thank you for helping me survive my youth."

There is another side to the tension and conflict of having a child who is different from you. It's having an *adult* who appreciates you for allowing exploration and growth in this area of personal decision making.

Thank you for engaging with this book. I hope it will help you survive the youth of your young person.

1

Family and
Emotional Issues

The adolescent and preadolescent years are a very special and unusual time. They transform your offspring from dependent child
to autonomous adult. These are years of exploration and, often,
of rebellion. Your children must decide for themselves which of their
childhood values are good and worthy of being held onto, and which of
their childhood presumptions need to be examined and challenged.
This is a very dramatic process! And now added to this volatile mix is
vegetarianism or veganism!

There is no need to be alarmed, no need to feel that this signals the
breakdown of everything you have worked so hard to create in your
household. This is not a catastrophe. Remember, childhood is a time for
change! Change in children is inevitable. You don't have to change, but
you should meet them halfway.

The very way a family is structured may make it feel difficult to meet
them halfway. Two methods can help: I call them "the tuba principle"
and "the Sleeping Beauty approach." But before I introduce these methods to you, let me identify why it is that you may have experienced your
child's veg*nism as alarming or catastrophic, as the breakdown of something important to your household.

Rearing children requires that a system be in place—children must
be fed and clothed; they need a place and time to sleep and play. Gro-
ceries must be brought, food prepared, bills paid, beds made. When we
are children the system serves us. It directs us toward maturity by having

rules and boundaries, and when it works, it insures that we are fed and rested. At some point we acquire tasks in the system, gradually assuming a more active role in making decisions about our own lives. When we are teenagers the balancing act of being taken care of and participating in decision making tilts toward the latter or is pushed there by our need to separate from the system.

A family evolves a system that provides rules and roles and, in doing so, achieves balance. Any change in one part of the system will provoke changes in another part. Because of this, huge changes don't have to occur to alter the whole system. No matter the magnitude of a change, any real, substantive change—especially ones that arise during a time of change for the family anyway, like the maturing of an adolescent—can change the whole system.

There are, in fact, two kinds of change. One kind is like switching playing pieces in a chess game but keeping the underlying rules the same. An example of this for a family might be when a child grows up. He may change from a pawn to a rook, but the rules of the game remain the same. All the same moves are made; the same responses are elicited. A second-order change, in contrast, changes the basic rules of the game: chess is no longer played in the same way. Your child's decision to become a veg*n may seem to her a simple change, say, from being a pawn to being a rook. But you know she is changing the rules of the game. Specifically, she is rejecting some basic rules of the house: "This is what we eat"; "This is what a holiday meal is"; "This is how we honor our ancestors, our culture, our parents"; "My way is right"; "This is how I do it." Convenience and custom are compelling aspects of any system: "I do it this way because it works." All of these responses reveal that veg*nism is a second-order change because our responses refer to fundamental ways we organize our world—what we eat, how we celebrate, how authority works.

In response to a second-order change, we may intensify the pressure on the person who is not conforming to the old system. We might start saying how important it is that the young person conform to the family system—someone's feelings are at stake, or a family tradition is being threatened, or he is rejecting someone or something. If this attempt to bring him back into the system doesn't work, we might remove all the support that could be brought to maintain the person he is trying to be, to pressure him into returning to the person he was. This pressure upon your child will feel almost unbearable. (We are very powerful, after all!) Yes, your child's decision does require a lot of real adjustments in the way a family operates. Yes, veg*nism strikes at the very foundation of your family. But the family system can survive a change such as this. It's okay to take it ad hoc, step by step.

I once read an analysis of the fairy tale "Sleeping Beauty" that I found immensely helpful in relating to my own children. After Sleeping Beauty pricks her finger on the spinning wheel and falls into a deep sleep, vines with thorns grow all around the wall of the town. The thorns represent the difficult moods and reactions of the adolescent as he or she separates from the parents and becomes an adult. Just as, after time, the thorny vines become roses, so will our adolescents awaken from their adolescence and be in full bloom as adults. Whenever I feel particularly frustrated and rebuffed by my teenagers, I remember that "This is their thorny period."

For you, the vegetarianism or veganism of your teenager may feel like those thorns. They keep you away from your child. They are a barrier, and a prickly one! But imagine that your child's vegetarianism is the beginning of the blossoming of her adult values. After all, your child is not rejecting your values. She is manifesting a level of sensitivity and tenderness toward the feelings of living creatures, her own health, or that of the environment. You must be the person who shaped these values.

Remember that a judgmental tone is an aspect of adolescence. The tone and shouting is the way a teenager tries to equalize the power between herself and her very powerful parents. We may feel impatient or furious when a teenager announces an ultimatum, dismisses our concerns, or uses a tone of disdain in speaking with us, especially when challenging something we hold special. But be careful with your feelings. Even when we feel frustrated with our children, we know that an adolescent's tone of voice or shouting doesn't actually equalize power. So don't become susceptible to these thorns. Remember they are growing inside. Speak to them calmly and evenly. *Listen.* Ask them, "What are you feeling?" Always let them know you will listen.

Your kids are emulating the ideas of thinkers such as Gandhi and Thoreau. Praise them for taking an ethical stand. Ask your child to tell you the process he went through in deciding to become a vegetarian and don't feel that he is judging you in his statements. Don't force him to eat meat. Don't tell him, "Well, just pick out the meat." Respecting him, even in his disagreements with you, teaches him the lesson of respect. You will discover this lesson blossoming in his life in many ways. He will have learned it from you.

If you are the type of parent who would schlep across town so your child can take tuba lessons, then do the same thing here—allow her to explore what it means to be a veg*n. Like tuba playing, she may not keep it up. Like tuba practicing, it may be inconvenient and even at times disturbing to the peace of the household. But like tuba playing, it is hers to explore and to be responsible for.

When things get tough or tense at home, imagine the veg*n child carrying a tuba. How would you help her? Do no less in this situation.

You may feel their veg*nism is about you, but it really isn't—no more than a tuba-playing child is. Even if your adolescent wants you to take his diet personally, as a reproach of what you are doing, you don't need to interpret it this way. You can say to yourself, "My child has decided to explore a different way of eating." There need not be any emotional content to that statement. It need carry neither judgment nor shame.

This change need not be your change. But you need to let it be hers for as long as it remains meaningful to her. This is what I mean by "the tuba principle." It means we meet our children's best impulses where they are and walk with them on their path. If possible, we try to anticipate what could assist them, but we don't try to pull them onto our path. Sure, our path is comfortable. We know it well. But, then, it is our path, not our child's.

Discomfort may well be an aspect of good parenting. Their path calls them. Their path is not the path of illegal activity and dishonest relationships. It is a path of high principle related to ethics or health. Don't stand in their way. If there are ways to help them, do so.

Remember Sleeping Beauty does awaken from her thorny period. This chapter will help you so that you don't feel you have to prune those thorns. Instead, you can identify a path through them. As with other things our kids introduce us to, we ourselves have our own parenting journey to follow. But, hey, we aren't the ones who have to carry the tuba!

ABUNDANCE/SCARCITY. The idea of giving up so many foods that are a part of your diet often prompts the question, "What's left to eat?" To take away meat may mean to you the loss of everything associated with the pleasures of eating. You see your diet as one of abundance, choice, and enjoyment. The veg*n diet strikes you as one of embracing scarcity, limitation, loss, deprivation, and diminishment. You are worried for your child, anticipating a sense of impoverishment for them. To your veg*n, however, who is bringing the natural enthusiasm of youth as well as the sense of many possible food choices, veg*nism is a diet of abundance.

In choosing to be supportive or unsupportive, parents provide their young person with the experience of either abundance or scarcity. If you say, "Pick out the meat," or "We're not fixing anything special for you," you guarantee that they will experience scarcity. Perhaps that makes their veg*nism easier on you, confirming in your mind that there really isn't anything good to eat on that diet.

But growing children need the feeling of abundance, not only in their food choices but also in their lives. They need to be both nourished and nurtured. They could benefit from your help in assuring a sense of abundance in their lives. What can you do?

- Help them experiment with many recipes to find the ones they—and you—really like.
- Help them experiment with lots of new vegetables and different spices.
- Help them eat a wide variety of foods.
- Help them find new kinds of food to eat.
- Help them learn how to make desserts.
- Consult the Vegetarian Food Guide (p. 106) and the Pantry List (pp. 75–77) for assistance in creating abundance.

ACCEPTANCE. During the ages of eight through thirteen, identity development involves two interrelated aspects of growth. The child does the inner work and then says through his or her actions, "This is who I am." Then the culture offers acceptance by saying to the child, "Yes, this is exactly who we wanted you to be." What occurs is a dialectic: the child presents; the culture affirms. They each refine their vision of who the child is becoming.

Erik Erikson offers the insight that the culture is doing a "double take"; the child becomes someone totally surprising, but also someone we recognize. Through its double take society says, "You are much different from who we thought you would be, but we recognize you and affirm you."

With veg*nism, your child is saying, "This is who I am." Our role in the dialectic is to affirm her, to mirror back to her the person she is becoming. "Yes, this is exactly who we wanted you to be." This response, of course, like so much of parent-child relationships at this time, does involve a double take: "My child, a veg*n?" As Erikson observes, we recognize the child, even though we are surprised. And our responsibility is to say back to her, "You are much different from who we thought you would be, but we recognize you and affirm you."

ACCESSIBILITY. We like to believe that our children are sharing their feelings and experiences with us. But as a wise college counselor said to me, "When students pack their suitcases to leave for college, they pack a lot more than clothes." That packing starts long before the end of the senior year. Surreptitious notes, jokes that we clearly don't get, emotional upheavals, gossip—the emotional life of an adolescent almost seems structured to exclude parents.

Yet with his diet your veg*n child is including you. We cannot meet our children in the school halls or other places where they are with their peers, but we can meet them here—in the kitchen and around the table. Don't pass up that chance. The baggage they leave with need not be conflict with parents regarding their decision about veg*nism.

ACCUSATION. Accusations involve painful encounters that attempt to lay blame or establish that someone has been wronged. Within families, they become ways in which we convey our opinions and establish our feelings, usually because we feel we are the one who has been wronged. Accusations not only cause pain, they reveal painful aspects of relationships.

Accusations may be raw or manipulative. An example of a raw accusation is a statement such as "You are doing this to ruin our lives." That statement implies that your child has a great deal of power over you, the adults in the house. Does she really have that much power? You may actually mean, "This is inconvenient, frustrating, infuriating!" Remember the tuba principle: you don't have to carry the tuba, and you don't have to be the one who lives as a veg*n. You only have to find a way to live with your veg*n. And that requires becoming more attuned to your emotions. Take the time to ask yourself, "Why am I feeling so furious, so frustrated, so inconvenienced? What expectations of mine are going unmet?"

Manipulative accusations often begin with "If you loved me . . ." You might be saying this because you feel rejected by your child or feel a sense of a loss of control over your child. For instance, you might find yourself saying things like "If you loved me you would . . . stop being a veg*n, . . . stop being so difficult, . . . stop talking about it, . . . start cooking for yourself."

What should you do when you hear these words? Your goal could be to find a way to change the dynamics between you and your child rather than using accusatory language, with its implicit or explicit desire to change behavior. Instead of "If you loved me . . ." you can say, "It is hard for me to relate to your new needs as a veg*n. Can we identify ways for you to take more responsibility in the kitchen?" or "I want to know what you are thinking and feeling, but it is difficult at times to hear what you are saying. Can we postpone this discussion to a different time when I can be more attentive?" Remember, they should not be required to love us by becoming who *we* think they should be.

On the other hand, you might be hearing your child say, "If you loved me" because they feel rejected by you and sense that they have no control. An adolescent vacillates between separation and neediness. Their veg*nism incorporates both ends of this continuum. They establish a separate identity through their veg*nism, but they still have a neediness to be loved by you, accepted in who they are becoming. If you hear your child say: "If you loved me you would . . . watch this video with me; . . . take me to the animal rights meetings; . . . stop eating dead animals," you are hearing the voice of a child who is separating from you but still in relationship to you. You are a very powerful person in his life. He is still needy, and perhaps distressed by a very alienating outside world. You need not get defensive when you hear "If you loved me" in relationship to his veg*nism; rather, assure him of your love. You can respond by saying: "When did you start thinking I don't love you?"

Remember, they are saying, "I am needy in this area, I need your love. I need your support." You can say, "We love you. You are changing. We will support you as you change, but that may not mean that we also change." And if you would take them across town for a tuba lesson, do the same thing here, take them across town for an animal rights meeting or to a natural foods store.

AFFECTION. You want your child to feel she can turn to you and that she can trust you. And you want her to feel generally warm toward you. You don't want her to feel cold-hearted. Entries in this chapter on "Listening," "Acceptance," "Attention," and "Hugs" offer suggestions on ways to convey affection.

ANGER. You may feel anger at your child for not following your advice, for not being like you, for insulting you, for expecting you to cater to this new and apparently strange diet, for taking time you don't have to fix food for him, or for seemingly ruining a holiday by refusing food lovingly prepared by a relative. This anger can fill a lot of your self. It can become self-righteous. It can lead you to say, "I told you so," or "You should have listened to me." These are words that are painful in the saying and in the hearing. And what if you did tell him so? His job is to find out what he knows, to exercise judgment, to learn what he is capable of doing. Failure and disappointment are aspects of his learning process.

It's not just that you are angry with him. He is angry with you. Why are you demanding that he eat something he cannot bear to eat?

Anger and disappointment are great burdens.

During times of confrontations it may be hard to remember, but her anger may be a healthy sign of independence, of framing a concern from her point of view. So, what happens when you are angry at her and she is angry at you? It is up to you to break the impasse. Remember, you are the adult here. The best way to respond is through mental preparation—you need to accept that it is actually age-appropriate behavior for your child to cause you to feel anger at her. If you expect it, you will perhaps not be trapped by feelings of anger. But if you do find yourself being angry, don't feel you have to give an immediate response or answer. One of the things that keeps anger circulating is the speed of the response. Take several deep breaths. Count backward from fifty. Say, "We can talk about this later but right now I need to be alone." Or "I want to honor your concern. I know you are upset. But I am, too, and I want to find a way to hear you without becoming angry myself. Let's take some time and come back to this topic again." Even so, no matter how angry you are, always assure them of your love: "I want you to know I love you, and that we can find a way to address this. It just can't be right now."

Perhaps the anger he feels toward the meat-eating world is both incomprehensible and frightening to you. It is very intense, and its intensity itself seems strange, even scary. It is hard to listen to him when he is angry without feeling damned by his statements. There is a way to listen to *and* through this anger. But it requires that you not feel threatened by your young person's anger or frustration. You can say, "It must be hard to be this angry," and wait for him to respond. You can help him to think about the relationship between powerlessness and anger. "It must be hard to care this much and not be able to change the world immediately." You can help him recognize that a certain degree of anger will probably always coexist with living in a way different from the majority of the culture, but that there are ways to focus the anger so that one isn't drowning in it. You can ask, "Now that you know this makes you angry, what is your next step?"

Together you might find ways to identify what specifically causes anger on your behalf and on hers. It is okay to ask her to be sensitive to those issues that make you angry, and for you to promise to be more sensitive to those issues that make her angry.

Anger is helpful—it teaches us something is wrong; but anger that doesn't help us grow isn't teaching us anything. (See also "Listening" and "Acceptance.")

ANTIESTABLISHMENT. Through veg*nism, is your child simply rebelling, being antiestablishment, questioning the actions and mores of the older generation? Well, yes and no.

Our children, because of our efforts and those of our own parents, experience the world differently from the way we do. For instance, to them "life in the fast lane" might carry the connotations of sixty-hour work weeks, little leisure, a world oriented toward consumption, a rushed, hectic, unable-to-slow-down world. Perhaps this is a world that doesn't appeal much to you either.

Veg*nism may represent a desire to establish a different relationship to the world and to the self. Taking time to cook, being informed as a consumer, being thoughtful about other living beings, these may be values that are very important to your young person. She is rejecting unthinking consumption of fast food. And she isn't the only one. The "slow cooking" movement, started in Italy, which advocates taking the time to cook meals well, also represents efforts to challenge a prevailing worldview. Yours may be one of the families in this country trying to be intentional about cooking and eating and spending time together.

Your young person may also be antiauthoritarian in other ways, too. He is exploring important political views. He is trying to figure out how to relate to current political structures. If these are hard things for your family to talk about, you can request that discussions about these issues not occur over dinner, and offer to listen to his ideas at a different time.

ARGUMENTS. Young people are ready to argue about numerous things. This is related to a developmental stage: the ability to think abstractly about issues. This cognitive ability enables them to engage energetically with issues such as "What is love?" "What is my relationship to others, to nonhuman nature?" "Does God exist?" These questions may seem argumentative and the arguments that ensue may seem frustrating, but really, this is such a healthy step! In contradicting us, talking back to us, and becoming "know-it-alls," our children are discovering that they, too, know things. They are not empty receptacles for others' thoughts and beliefs.

Even though veg*nism appears to give them a ready platform for arguing, it is actually giving them a way to focus both hypothetical and logical reasoning. (See also "Conversations.")

ATTENTION. A great French religious writer, Simone Weil, observes that, "Those who are unhappy have no need for anything in this world but people capable of giving them attention." She then provides directions on how to give attention: "The love of our neighbor in all its fullness simply means being able to say to him: 'What are you going through?'" The British novelist and philosopher Iris Murdoch explained in *The Sovereignty of Good* that what Weil meant is "the idea of a just and loving gaze directed upon an individual reality." Such attention, Murdoch urges, is "the characteristic and proper mark of the active moral agent." Murdoch continues, "The more . . . [it is] seen that another . . . has needs and wishes as demanding as one's own, the harder it becomes to treat a person as a thing." Between them, Weil and Murdoch offer parents a blueprint for parenting preadolescents and adolescents: bringing attention to each of them as having needs and wishes as demanding to them as ours are to us; asking of them simply and honestly, "What are you going through? I love you and I'd like to know."

AUTHORITY. You may be wondering, is veg*nism a challenge to your authority as a parent? Some parents believe so, and respond by saying, "Absolutely not. Not in my house. Not while you are still being fed by my wages. You cannot be a veg*n." By opening this book, you signal that you at least want to understand what your child is doing and perhaps try to meet them halfway.

The decision to become a veg*n is not really what many parents experience it as—a challenge to their authority, a judgment, a rebellion, a thwarting of the parent's plans and desires for a child. But your response to vegetarianism, if it is authoritarian and demanding, results in exactly what you mistook it for at first: rebellion. Your inflexibility or judgmental response creates the environment for the child to react against it: Now she needs to rebel, to thwart you, to judge you because her ethical or health stance directs her in the opposite direction than your will. Because you are, to her, acting impetuously, unlovingly, inflexibly, you become like the Greek gods—having power but not true influence. You become that which she truly has to move away from. Your behavior in relation to her decision-making process about vegetarianism will determine whether you, like the gods of Olympus, will be toppled from authority.

Have you noticed you protect something all the more rigidly precisely because your child opposes it or rejects it? It is a natural but perverse instinct to protect our authority, but usually we recover our equanimity and think, "How important is this actually to me?" So the question becomes, how important is meat to you? Or dairy products and eggs? Is it a convenience to eat these foods? There is, of course, nothing wrong with convenience. Is it enjoyable? Probably. Is it necessary? Not really. This is the pressure point where your child is challenging you. It is okay for you to maintain that eating these foods is necessary for you, but it is helpful if you can acknowledge that it is not necessary for your child.

A guide to the SAT advises that any answers that use the phrases "always," "must," "never," "cannot," etc. are usually the wrong answers. Isn't this true for so much in life, especially parenting? If we answer our children with these words we are exercising our authority, but what have we gained?

The key is to let them know that you trust them because children—especially adolescents—grow by being trusted enough to make mistakes. This is how they learn from their decision-making process. It is a much harder job to allow them to make mistakes than it is simply to tell them what to do.

How can they grow in decision making if their only decision is whether to listen to you and respect what *you* think should be done? As an adult, you know that some of your toughest decisions involve heeding your moral center when in the midst of what are the gray areas of life. Allowing your child to be a veg*n allows him to determine what is his moral center, not yours. Maybe it will stay central to him, maybe it won't. It is part of his task to determine that; don't complicate the issue by deciding the issue is your authority.

Remember, children will always use their parents as references for their actions and for support until they have matured to be their own grounding force. You want to be experienced as sufficiently nonjudgmental to continue to be someone your child approaches for wisdom and advice as he moves along the path of determining what works for him.

To absolutely oppose something means that all his explorations of that "something" will occur outside your sphere of influence. Is that what you really want? I have met many young adults on campus who had to wait to become vegans until they went to college. Where was the person who could help them begin to study minimum daily requirements or develop new comfort foods to ease the alienation or loneliness of the first year of college? That person had said, "Not in my house!"

Veg*nism is not unethical or immoral behavior. It is not even dangerous. But if you banish it from the house or disapprove in other ways, you may cut yourself off from an important part of your child's life.

BENEFITS. You are quite aware of the downside of your child's veg*nism, including its inconvenience. But take a moment to consider the benefits. Veg*nism is an opportunity for your child to become more involved in the kitchen (see "Chores" in chapter 2). Not only does this prepare him for independence (it's coming sooner than he realizes), but it may create a positive time of sharing for you when you are both in the kitchen. Perhaps you will help him interpret a recipe or learn a new ingredient. In addition, your health (yes, *your* health) may improve. Even if the rest of the family doesn't adopt a vegetarian diet, chances are everyone will be exposed to some new foods and more plant-based meals. Parents might find that their cholesterol levels start to drop if there are more soyfoods, more veggies, and a little less meat in their diet. And mothers of a certain age who are coping with menopause symptoms may find that incorporating soyfoods into family recipes provides some relief. Certain evidence suggests that compounds in soybeans are useful for relieving these symptoms.

BLAME. Sometimes veg*nism becomes the stock reason for something going wrong. Tensions between you and your child? It's her veg*nism. Another child becomes veg*n? It's your veg*n child's fault. It may seem easier if there is someone to blame for tension or for another's change; this makes the tension or the change more comprehensible. Even if your child were a meat eater, there would probably be tensions between you. Veg*nism is just the way those tensions are experienced right now. It is not the *content* of the dispute that is pertinent here (that is, that the dispute is about veg*nism), it is the *process of relating between* *generations* (which undergoes enormous changes during your child's growth through adolescence). Similarly, a second child may be interested in veg*nism for reasons specific to that child; her process has brought her to a similar content decision as your other child, but it has been her own individual process. Watch out for targeting veg*nism for blame when the issues may be more complex.

CHANGE. "Just because my child has changed, why should *I* change?" Well, you don't have to. Except, of course, that each of us is always changing. Yesterday we were different from who we are today. And tomorrow we will be different from today. That is the nature of being alive.

But why should anyone consciously change? Because we want something to be brought into our lives that is absent from it; because the way we lived yesterday pointed us toward something today. Often the real question is, "Why should I change just because you have?" Or "Why should I change when the change being required of me is inconvenient, frustrating, uncomfortable, or difficult?" Well, isn't that one aspect of any definition of parenting? Getting my teenage son to early morning band practice was inconvenient and frustrating. Why should *I* have had to change? Because it was important to my son and they were more benefits than drawbacks to adapting to his need.

Yes, you need to change. However, you don't need to become a vegan or a vegetarian. You simply need to accept that you are a *parent* of a vegan or a vegetarian. The issue of change is actually two questions, "What is his reality and how do I fit into it?" and "What is my reality and how does he fit into it?"

COMMUNICATION. Rita Boothby, author of *The Golden Rules of Parenting: For Children and Parents of All Ages*, points out that much parent-child communication fits into "four corners of the same box: Criticism, Orders, Teasing, and Endless Instruction." Children, however, benefit from other forms of communication that are characterized by Interest, Openness, and Affection. You want your children to feel they can turn to you and that they can trust you. (For specifics on communication see "Conversations.")

COMMUNITY. One aspect of maturation is the evolution of awareness that we are connected not only to other family members but to an entire community. We move from being self-centered, and then family-centered, to being community-centered. A sense of responsibility to this larger community often accompanies the awareness of our interconnectedness. If your young person is a veg*n for ethical or environmental reasons, she has expanded her sense of responsibility to the larger community and determined that this larger community includes not only humans but nonhumans and nature. This sense of connection and responsibility to the larger community is something that you can praise.

COMPASSION. Recent philosophical movements have rooted ethics in feelings of sympathy and compassion. Experiencing sympathy, it is argued, is a complex intellectual as well as emotional exercise—an exercise of the imagination that requires self-consciousness, comparison, judgment, and evaluation. Philip Mercer, in *Sympathy and Ethics*, explains: "It is not enough that I should imagine how *I* should feel if *I* were in the other person's place; I have to imagine how [the other] feels." Morality and justice, according to these theorists, require first having sympathy. The philosopher Arthur Schopenhauer explains that one understands another's pain through "the everyday phenomenon of *compassion*, of the immediate *participation* . . . in the *suffering* of another. . . . It is simply and solely this compassion that is the real basis of all *voluntary* justice and *genuine* loving-kindness." Schopenhauer continues, "Boundless compassion for all living things is the firmest and surest guarantee of pure moral conduct."

What does this have to do with parenting a veg*n child? In fact, several things. First, the directive for compassion—"I have to imagine how [the other] feels"—is an extremely helpful way to enable successful communication with your young person. Second, your young person may be motivated by compassion to care about what is happening to animals, and this compassion may have led to his veg*nism. You need not agree with your child's ethical reasoning to respond with compassion to your child's compassion. But understanding his motivations may help you acknowledge that your child has progressed to a new level of growth, one that can grapple with ethical issues and make decisions.

CONFLICT. The closer the parent-child relationship, the more likely that dietary differences will bear the burden of many nondietary conflicts. Any unresolved aspects of the relationship may attach themselves to veg*n/meat-eating dynamics. The tensions may be caused by something else but find expression in discussions and debates about food choices. Your meat eating and her vegetarianism become burdened with representing basic relationship issues—issues of control, especially. The debate might appear to be about what was eaten at supper, but it may actually be about something entirely different. Our children need our love even when they are in conflict with us. We have to find ways of loving them *through* the conflict. If we cannot find ways in which their veg*nism can be a cause of growth of the parent-child relationship per se, we need to find ways, at the minimum, for there to be steadiness in love at this time. Expect conflict, and you won't be surprised by it. (See also "Anger.")

CONTROL. As parents, there is a part of us that wants only the best for our child or children. We feel such a deep tenderness for their vulnerability and a desire to keep them safe and happy. But there is another part that feels frustration, anger, even intolerance, with this same child's willfulness or resistance to something we desire for him. We think, "How could he want this. . . ?" and we may be possessed by an accompanying irrational fury. We discover a desire to bring the child under control again. Perhaps we "put our foot down" and say, "Absolutely not!" We say, "I told you not to . . ." "I will not even listen to this . . ." "Not in my house!"

After the controlling part of us has prevailed, treating the child rudely, unlovingly, the loving part of us may surface again and be aghast at the controlling parent who ignored vulnerability and imposed control. When this happens with me, I ask myself, "Why did I do that?" Not only that, but "What did I think I was losing so that I had to do that?" I feel like an elephant who crushed a flea, because now I have been reminded of the power I always have as a parent. My willful, controlling self is in conflict with my nurturing, loving self. When I realize I have done this, I approach my child, apologize, and try to explore what happened.

As the parent of a child who has stopped eating meat (and perhaps also dairy and eggs), you are bound to discover that these different selves feel unreconciled. The important thing is to become aware of which one wins in relationship with your child and ask yourself why. We can learn new ways of relating to children. As parents we must find in ourselves the part that wants the best for our children and develop its strengths so that it is not overpowered by the controlling part that thinks it always know best. Rather than dictating to our children who they can be, we need to create an openness to the person each is becoming.

CONVERSATIONS. Jump-starting conversations with your young person is made easier by asking open-ended questions such as:
"I've been thinking about what you said about . . ."
"You were telling me about your idea for . . ."
"I was wondering if things are going any better with . . ."
You are telling her through questions such as these that you want to hear about who she is, not who *you* think she should be. In response to her answers, you must observe the basic ground rule of effective conversation: no accusations, no blame, no jumping in with *your* answers.

Conversations about how your young person is doing with his veg*nism require compassion. Signaling to your child that you care about what he is experiencing by making statements such as, "It can be hard to be different," or "It can be difficult to be so angry," can be a sign to your child that you empathize with his situation and that you can listen.

CRUELTY. Your child may be struggling with the fact that an enormous amount of cruelty is inflicted on domestic animals who are eaten. You may have responded to this struggle by thwarting her veg*nism, or by not caring if she has anything to eat at the family table, or by giving ultimatums, or by saying, "You *have* to eat meat." Or perhaps, like one family, your family may go to great lengths to frustrate your child. When that young person "adopted" a turkey to support at a farm sanctuary, the family tried everything possible to buy that specific turkey and have that turkey butchered for their Thanksgiving dinner. Another young person reported to me that when she was thirteen and newly vegetarian, a friend of her parents offered her tortellini salad, saying it was vegetarian. After she had eaten it he laughed as if he had played a marvelous trick on her and told her the tortellini was filled with veal.

What do experiences like this teach? They may confirm your child's viewpoint that people who eat animals are cruel. She or he is experiencing that cruelty from family and friends.

The alternative is to respond to your young person's concern about cruelty to animals by saying, "I can see that you care very deeply about this. There are things we as a family can do to support you short of becoming veg*ns ourselves." You might agree to designate an animal sanctuary to support, or expand your menu to include a veg*n meal once in a while.

CULT. Is veg*nism a cult? No. Will your child fall in with groups of people who use drugs and are involved in other illegal activities? Not because he or she is veg*n. Some aspects of veg*nism may feel cultlike to you, especially your young person's seeming obsession with inquiring into the contents of every dish offered to him or her. Yes, there are some bands that are veg*n and have veg*n lyrics; there are some veg*ns who have tattoos. But veg*nism does not evolve as a group identity as much as an individual pilgrimage. Veg*nism has been adopted by famous people and everyday people, Republicans and Democrats, philosophers and athletes. Some people first become vegetarian at age fifty-five or sixty or seventy, some at twelve, or eight, or six. Sometimes parents became veg*ns first. Don't assume the worst about your young person but the best. You can ask her to describe how she decided to stop eating meat, or if applicable why she decided to stop using animal products. Her responsiveness and her answers may reassure you that veg*nism is not a cult.

DOOR SWINGS OFF THE HINGES. Family therapists have a metaphor for times when immense change and conflict occur in a family: "the door swings off the hinges." Your child is changing; you are trying to survive this changing.

During the year that our door swung off the hinges, I tried to identify exactly what was the quality of that unhinging: Is it that we, parent and child, are both pushing on the same door from opposite directions and it becomes unhinged? That was part of it. Is it that we are used to everyone using the door from our side, and so it opens our way, but the transition to adulthood means that the child rehangs the door so that it opens outward, from his or her point of view, into their new world? This was true, too.

If you experience the immense conflicts that can occur when a child is between sixteen and eighteen, try to avoid doing anything absolute at the time except around safety issues (drinking/drug use/driving/etc.). You don't want the door to swing back and hit you. These years are supposed to set that door a-swinging. Be careful, so that when it's done swinging you and your college-age child can re-hang the door.

EATING TOGETHER GROUND RULES. Preparing and serving food in a relaxed way is an approach to family tensions that can put everyone involved at ease. Our relationship to food when we are eating needs to be casual and relaxed. Most of us, young and old, parent or child, don't want to hear a lecture during dinner. Establish the ground rule that debates about the content of the meal, whether it be meat or veg*n, are off-limits, and discussing the ideas of meat eating or veg*nism during dinner is also off-limits. And require that everyone follow these ground rules. Create dinnertime as a demilitarized zone. School, work, the day's events, plans, memories—this is enough material for any family to discuss!

EMBARRASSMENT. You may feel embarrassed about your child's veganism when you are talking with or are eating with friends and relatives. It may feel awkward as he refuses foods. You may be asked directly by a friend, "Isn't it embarrassing to go out to eat?"

How do you handle your feelings and those of other adults? The first question that arises is, Why is it embarrassing? Why is your child's decision seen as reflecting negatively on you? This is usually because we often don't know how to respond to difference. But differences need not be embarrassing. Your friend may have vicariously imagined conflict and drama and is seeking from you confirmation of his imaginative construction of your family dynamics. But even if you are embarrassed by your child, you need not confirm your friend's assumptions. Why does it matter to him? Because many people are comforted by learning of another's troubles.

You could begin by saying, "I am proud of my child. There are ways to handle every situation. He is teaching me ways to do that. I am learning from him." You invert embarrassment by responding gracefully, with pride for your child.

While you are worried about how your child's dietary changes may prove embarrassing when eating with friends and relatives, remember that you have much more power to embarrass your child than your child does to embarrass you. After all, among other things, you changed his diapers! Most young people are very concerned about how their parents will embarrass them. Don't use their dietary changes as tools for embarrassment. Avoid saying things like, "How can she (or he) enjoy this food?" or "Look at her picking at her vegetables. . . ." or "That was back when she used to eat real food." Don't call attention to her decision.

Some children prefer to be ignored rather than in the spotlight. Don't make their decision painful to them. (See also "Third-Person Communication.")

EMOTIONS/FEELINGS. We like to try to move through the world unalarmed. The information your child is trying to tell you about his reasons for veg*nism can be pretty alarming. You may feel you are losing control of your emotional space. What can you do? Tell your offspring that you hear her, that you understand that she is concerned about the experience of animals. If you are willing, assure her that you are willing to read one pamphlet on the subject. Ask her to research what is available and pick one thing on the subject for you to read. (You might agree that reading chapter 4 of this book is a way to address her concerns.) (See also "Anger" and "Fears.")

ENGAGEMENT. Through engagement, we encourage our children. We can do this by asking questions such as, "What do you have to do to be a healthy veg*n?" "What is your next step?"

EXPLANATIONS. You and your young person both understand the origins of her or his veg*nism. You simply have different understandings. Your daughter or son says, "I object to killing animals," or "Animal products are unhealthy," or "Meat production is destroying the environment!" You may be thinking, "My son is rebelling against the family," or "My daughter has an eating disorder," or "This is a fad," or "He's joined a cult!" or "She has always been so sentimental!"

How do you reconcile your explanations? One way is to challenge his decision. Another way is to decide to listen to him and find out what he is thinking. Is your explanation adequate once you have listened to his thoughts and beliefs?

FADS. You might be telling yourself that children will go through fads, and this is one of them. Don't tell her this is a phase that she'll outgrow, even if you believe that it is. This tells her you see her as being childish. She wants to be respected, not patronized. Young people have told me that it has been a very disturbing experience to hear their parents refer to their dietary change as a "fad." You might wish it to be a fad, something that is passed through quickly, but for your child it is a stage of growth.

It is the nature of growth toward adulthood to try on various activities and beliefs. Even if what he is trying on lasts only for a short period, to him it is exploration, not a fad. Moreover, with veg*nism, many young people see their decision as a moral one. Belittling it by calling it a fad belittles your child.

FAILURE. Do we think we are failures if our diet is rejected? Do we find a security in being needed by our children? There is much we can do to encourage our children to fail at being vegetarians and vegans. Why do we use our energy in this way, blocking their desires? Do we want them (secretly) to fail in order to prove that we are right (confirming our superior knowledge and experience); that they need us (we have to help them with their food choices or they will fail), thus proving, as well, our irreplaceability? Through their failure do we show that we parents can't be replaced and neither, for that matter, can meat or dairy? Why encumber your relationship with your child with an unnecessary use of power? Save the power for when it is really needed. Instead of encouraging failure, help your child out.

FEARS. You may be worried about your child:

- I am worried about her health.
- I am worried he is going to die.
- I am worried that he will have a hard time being a vegetarian (a worry you ironically fulfill if you oppose his decision).
- I worry what others will do in response.
- I worry that she will be rejected by her peers.

You have these fears because you love your child. I hope that this book will relieve you of some of these fears.

You might be worried about yourself:

- I am worried that I will have to learn how to cook new things.
- I am worried that I have to shop for new items.
- I am worried that I have to cook two meals.
- I worry about how I will explain it to the relatives.

Anxiety is uncomfortable and you may wish to disallow or limit veg*nism because your feelings about vegetarianism are uncomfortable to you. Why not sit down with your child and share your fears with her? Tell her you aren't trying to change her decision, but you want to find ways to address these issues. You might consult chapter 3 first, so that you have addressed your fears about nutrition and dispelled those fears that are ungrounded.

GENDER ISSUES. Some members of your family may feel that is it not masculine for a young man to be caring and compassionate. His veg*nism becomes an opportunity to taunt him, calling him various insults. You can assist your young person by gently reminding others that it is not polite to call names. You can also point out that sympathy and compassion are ethical responses to suffering.

GRANDPARENTS and other extended family. Grandparents, aunts, and uncles may say, "You must put your foot down and stop this!" or "Who does he think he is?" How do you reframe the issue for grandparents who see vegetarianism as disobedience? First, discourage dinnertime conversations, arguments, and defenses. If the decision isn't constantly being brought into the conversation, the sense of rebellion that is being attributed to it may fade into the background. Second, advocate on behalf of your young veg*n with your extended family. Don't become part of the alliance against him. Your parents are not allowing you to be the parent here but feel a need to interfere. Simply reassure them, "this is nothing to worry about." (But also see "'Hands Off' as Much as Possible," advice— at this point—for your parents as well as you!)

For grandparents or other relatives who are concerned about your child's health on a veg*n diet, you need not get into a debate. Give them a copy of the American Dietetic Association's Position Statement on Vegetarian Diets. You can get this from the Web at www.eatright.org or by calling the ADA at 1-800-877-1600.

Finally, you set the tone. If you are relaxed and affirming about your child's decision, you will teach your parents and others to be, too.

"GROW UP." Being matter of fact about animals' deaths is a sign of health and maturity in our culture. Our culture equates growing up with growing out of a childlike sense of animals as our peers; it views caring for animals as being sentimental, not only childish ("Don't be such a baby," "Act your age") but feminine as well. As individuals, we grow up learning to deny the legitimacy of our feelings. Thus you may believe

that your young person's veg*nism is a problem of misplaced or imma-
ture emotions: your young person is just too sensitive; she never got over
those Disney movies; she doesn't accept loss; she doesn't know how
properly to focus her emotions on "real" problems.

Besides "Grow up," boys and young men may hear statements such
as "Be a man," or "Don't be a sissy." The assumption being made in these
statements is that *not* caring is a sign of maturity and so caring about
animals is a sign of arrested development. This assumption is partly
rooted in the mistaken assumption that morality is not based on compassion. But being an adult or being a "man" and caring can go hand in
hand. Your young person may be trying to show just how it is done. (See
"Compassion.")

"HANDS OFF" AS MUCH AS POSSIBLE. With adolescents,
it is hard to know what is *your* issue and what is *their* issue; what you absolutely have to step on and redirect and what you need to leave alone. A
wise counselor advised me in regard to my own two children: "hands off
as much as possible." We have to allow our children to experiment and
grow. We have to allow them to make wrong choices so that they learn
the process of making good choices.

You can say, "All right, you may try this. But let's discuss how you are
going to get your calcium, protein, etc., and how this can be integrated
into the family's routines without too much disruption. What do you
propose?"

HUGS. Whenever possible, give your child, even your teen, a hug.
Perhaps there has been a confrontation, perhaps you are both tired, perhaps old issues have been recycled under the guise of discussing
veg*nism. This is the time for a hug, and a parent is the best equipped
to initiate a hug. Children may grudgingly accept it, give you just their
shoulder or the side of their body to receive the hug, but they get the
message. You enclose them in your love. You can say, "This is a challenge. We've never had to do something exactly like this before. It requires forethought, and sometimes we are tired. Sometimes we make
mistakes. But we love you."

HUMOR. We can survive our kids' changes, their interests—and so can
they! A lighthearted response assures you both of that. It relieves tensions
and teaches your child how to respond to change in a nonthreatening way.

You can say, "Well, at least you haven't given up chocolate!" Responding with humor, especially after a tense interaction, reassures your young person that you continue to be connected, continue to be moving forward through an entangled relationship.

But don't use humor as a way to lampoon them. Jokes should not be at their expense. Then you are being cruel. (See "Teasing.")

"I'M NOT GOING TO FIX ANYTHING EXTRA." Perhaps you declare this because you simply don't have time to fix anything extra. Perhaps it is a way of punishing your veg*n child or of reducing the rewards of veg*nism. Perhaps you are uneasy abdicating responsibility for her meal; maybe you don't want someone else cooking in your kitchen. Whatever the reasons motivating this declaration, it becomes a way of maintaining control at the expense of your child's health. For instance, if dinner is green beans and meat loaf, your child is left with only green beans. Now is the time to sit down with your child and discuss menu planning. She needs your support and she needs nourishment. (See the Vegetarian Food Guide in chapter 3.)

IMPATIENCE. Your young person is old enough to envision an ideal world but perhaps not experienced enough to recognize the innumerable barriers to achieving that world. Young veg*ns envision a world without meat eating. And the way to achieve it is by getting everyone they know to stop eating meat. Because they see every piece of meat as representing an individual animal, each meal that is meatless is a movement toward that ideal world. The world they want to create cannot come into existence immediately. But that is so hard to hear and much harder to grasp. Be patient with their impatience. It may not feel like it at the time, but their impatience is a sign of developmental growth.

"IN YOUR FACE" VEG*NISM. Their separation from us feels like rejection, never more so than when they are in our face about an issue they care about but we don't. Remind yourself: This is nothing unusual.

"IT'S THE AMERICAN THING." If you grew up in the United States, it may seem as though meat eating isn't just the natural thing to do but the American thing to do. In the nineteenth century, immigrants actually underreported the amount of meat they ate when writing back to their families in Europe because they didn't think anyone would believe how much Americans ate! For your child to deviate from meat eating may seem "un-American," even unpatriotic.

If you are an immigrant to the United States, you may be concerned that by not eating meat your child will be rejected by the kids at his school because your child is not doing the "American" thing. You may be worried that your child's veg*nism will be the excuse for cruel racist/ethnic taunts.

For the homegrown American, the "American" thing of eating meat seems one of the givens of citizenship; for the immigrant American it seems the mantle of passing as an American. What actually may be motivating this concern is that you would like to protect your child from all the possible bad experiences of being "different." This is often an area where we as parents may have our own scars, our own feelings of powerlessness. But by recommending conformity to your child at the expense of your young person's evolving ethical sense of right and wrong, you suggest to your child that being accepted is more important than acting ethically.

Racist taunts are painful, but so is the feeling of having one's ethical motivations thwarted. Your child may also start protecting you from learning about racist incidents that happen that are unrelated to her choice of diet because she sees that it concerns you so.

For those who see eating meat as the American thing to do, it may be that a new generation is finding different ways to define "American." This is not unpatriotic; in fact, it, too, is the American way. United States history is steeped in reform movements that changed the status of women (who couldn't vote in federal elections until 1919), African Americans (who had been enslaved and then, once freed, discriminated against), and children (who once, by law, could work eight to twelve hours a day in factories and mines). This reform spirit is awakened in your child. In this spirit, you could think of his or her veg*nism as the American thing to do.

"IT'S THE END OF THE WORLD." Well, it isn't really, but it may feel like that. In fact, every day as our young people grow up, our world changes. Their interests change the way our world is structured. Whether their interests lead them toward a (very loud) musical instrument, or the desire to go to the mall, or the need to conduct scientific experiments at home, each time they develop a new interest our world changes. But your child's veg*nism may feel very different from the learning of a loud musical instrument, or an interest in hanging with friends at a mall. It may seem like the end of the world because meat or dairy is very important in your life or in the life of your family. You may truly wonder how you can adjust to this change. The answer is, you adjust to this change as you adjust to all of his changes, even the ones that are so incremental you might not have perceived them: day by day, step by step, with openness, and renegotiation of expectations and requirements. (See, for instance, "Chores" in chapter 2.)

It may feel like the end of the world because you are farmers, dairy producers, owners of a fast food franchise, or earn a living in other ways because people eat meat, dairy products, or eggs. Your child may now disagree with what you do professionally. But that is not the end of the world, either. It is appropriate to establish boundaries around topics that are off-limits; this may be one of them.

Maybe I am taking a figure of speech too literally. You may make this exclamation to convey that your child's veg*nism is such a radical change. Still, let her experience what this change means to her. After all, our world could never be her world.

LISTENING. I read once that the way to respond to a child who has scraped her knee or fallen from his bike is to think of yourself not as their parent but as their grandparent. The grandparent would most likely pull that child into his or her lap and say, "Oh, I am so sorry." The parent is more likely to say, "I warned you about that hill."

The art of listening to your child begins with recognizing that your child will let you know when he is comfortable talking with you. He is the one who has to initiate a conversation.

And when he does—and acknowledges self-doubts, worries, or tribulations, imagine yourself pulling him in to your lap. Hear his tribulations as a veg*n as though you were a loving, nonjudgmental grandparent. After your child signals that he wants to talk, concentrate on what he is saying and maintain eye contact with him. Empty yourself of expectations and demands. Don't hold onto an opinion that you need to express. Don't interrupt him. Don't feel you have to give any advice. Don't be judgmental. Avoid, too, body language that is judgmental in conversations: Don't lift your eyebrows or grimace, sigh, gasp, or take short breaths. Don't say, "Well, I warned you about that." (You might have, but so what?)

If you are willing to listen, this is an area where your child probably wants to engage you and tell you what she is learning, why she cares, what she is experiencing.

Ask open-ended questions: "What do you think?" "How are you do-ing?" "How did that feel?" Don't say, "I know how that feels."

If appropriate, you can say, "That must have hurt." Don't change the subject. Hear all your child has to say. Even if her complaint is about you, you can still say, "I am sorry that happened." You aren't saying you will change. You are listening to her. Stay calm. Overreaction alienates your young person. Often, we hear our children tell us something that troubles them and we want to solve it. But most of the time we don't need to. We simply need to listen.

LOVE. The bonds of love are all about respect and rejoicing in the other's discovery of who she or he is meant to be. Love enables self-dif-ferentiation. Self-differentiation is when one is part of a family and yet re-mains an individual. Love occurs when we let each member be who each is meant to be yet stay a part of the family as well. Take acceptance, affec-tion, compassion, listening, mix with "hugs," and as frequently as possible add "I love you," and you will guarantee not only love but growth. For love facilitates growth.

MIDLIFE CRISIS. Your child's veg*nism may enter your family's life right on the heels of a forty-something realization that you are not completely satisfied with your life. At the same time that you are examining your own goals and aspirations so, too, is your child exam-ining his. You see the promise in his life, but see your own as closed in. You see his vigor; and you are tired. You hear his optimism; where did yours go? His future seems limitless, yours limited. You see all the opportunities he has while feeling your own are foreclosed. You might think, "All these opportunities and my child picks this one to care about!"

It is important to recognize what is your issue and what is his issue. Your crisis of vision or purpose is not his crisis. If we realize that our thought patterns lead us in this direction, we need to redirect them. We need to say to ourselves, "What am I feeling?" Are you perhaps feeling jealous of your young person's freedom to choose and change? Are you feeling trapped not only by your own life but also by the assumptions that accompany your child's choices? That is, have you tired of being chief cook and bottle washer and now find that even more is expected of you? Once you identify your feelings, you can explore ways that your needs could be met (perhaps by seeing a counselor, using *What Color Is*

Your Parachute?, renegotiating kitchen chores, developing interests out-side of being a parent) without having your unresolved needs impinge on your young person's decisions.

MOTIVATION. It takes a great deal of motivation to be a veg*n. You may feel the desire to redirect this motivation. Why can't she feel moti-vated about . . . the SAT/getting into college/picking up her room/prac-ticing her instrument, and so forth? Because she doesn't. She has chosen this issue and she has made it her own. Sure, you can try wrenching it from her, but why not recognize what she cares about and see if that can help her recognize what you care about? Make a deal: "I know being a veg*n is important to you. Well, keeping your room picked up/finishing your college application/practicing your instrument, etc., is important to us. If you can help us feel more comfortable about this issue, we will support your veg*nism."

"MY DAD . . . , MY MOM. . . ." What is often elusive to us is how our children experience us, their parents. We often learn how our children view us as they talk about us to their peers. Then they are re-laxed, they don't need to have their "parent radar" on, editing their thoughts or being on edge because we might jump in and be judgmen-tal of them. We rarely are privy to these conversations, though, and so don't actually know how we are being experienced. But, at rare mo-ments, you may have a glimpse of this. One teen sent me his 'zine (a small alternative magazine), and it contained his "Vegan Recipe of the Month." He introduced it by saying, "My dad made this pasta dish for me recently." What a world of relationships is contained in that sen-tence! His father not only respected his veganism; he also cooked him a vegan dinner. I think the young man was very proud to include this recipe and the reference to his father. It was a double act of affirma-tion—first on the part of the father to the son, and then on the part of the son to the father.

In another 'zine, the author refers to a book that was very influential in her thinking, and says, "I got my dad to buy it for me when I got into college." Again, in one sentence, relationship, respect, and support are evoked. These references, and the countless other examples that could be given, are reminders that though our children are moving toward in-dependence, they truly are interdependent with us, their parents. Signs of love and support from us to them are so essential.

NEGOTIATION. You and your child are very different people. Why shouldn't this be the case? You were brought up by different people during different times. Many things have changed. It's okay that you and your young person are not the same. Veg*nism is only one aspect of this difference, but it may be the decision that crystallizes these differences. What should you do? Don't allow these differences to overwhelm your relationship. Agree to disagree.

You can say, "You see meat as murder. We don't. You don't have to eat it, but we will continue to do so." Or, "We have different opinions. We will respect your decision, and we need you to respect ours."

NEIGHBORS, FRIENDS, AND RELATIVES. You may wonder how you should explain your young person's decision to others. If you feel comfortable with her decision, you may say, "I am proud that Carrie has made an ethical decision and is figuring out how to live an ethical life." If you are not comfortable saying that, you can signal your acceptance of your child's decision simply by shrugging your shoulders and saying, "It is her decision. It's fine. But you'll need to ask Carrie about it." This conveys that you don't feel it has to be justified and that you aren't worried about it. After all, it really isn't anyone else's business. Remember the tuba principle. It's like saying, "Yes, my daughter plays the tuba." You support her and you aren't worried about her.

NOMAD YEAR. The senior year of high school is a year of transition. Your high-school senior is preparing to leave the home nest, to move from dependence to independence. Because a senior is and yet is not living at home, it helps to view this year as a "nomad year." Yes, they are home to get some sleep and refuel, but then they are off again—to go to school, attend extracurricular activities, and socialize with their friends. They may also be making college visits. Once my partner labeled our son's senior year his nomad year, we were freed from certain expectations. No, he probably wouldn't be home for supper. No, the room probably wasn't going to be picked up to our standards. Why should it be, since he wasn't really living in it? Lots of emotional reactions to your child's "disappearance" from the home scene may be felt. Be careful not to confuse these reactions to your young person's necessary transition to adulthood with your reactions to their veg*nism.

PEER ISSUES. Don't isolate your child emotionally because now a part of his anger may be turned toward you as a meat eater. It probably is turned toward his meat-eating peers as well. Indeed, when it comes to your child's vegetarianism, it is probably safe to assume that his friends and you—often on different sides of arguments—eerily agree. What does this mean for your child? He needs you even more.

We parents feel a strong urge to protect our children. We may be concerned about the cruelty of their peers. If we protect our children from negative experiences, we may be protecting them equally from positive experiences. Help them strategize how to respond to those who are uneasy with the issue. Ask them how things are going as a veg*n with their friends. Ask open-ended questions such as, "What did you think when they said that?" "What do you think you would want to do next time?" "What did that teach you about that situation?" I have written a book for veg*ns about interacting with meat eaters, *Living among Meat Eaters*. Many teens and college students have told me how useful it has been for their specific situations. Helping young people develop interpersonal skills is a terrific gift we give them as parents. Then, whether they have positive or negative experiences, they are still successful.

"PICK OUT THE MEAT." Your child cannot just "pick out the meat" from a dish. This is not inflexibility on her part. You are asking your child to violate her ethics. From your child's perspective, the entire dish is contaminated. Teenagers believe their issues are considered unimportant; advising them they can eat food even though it is contaminated confirms this for them. If this issue—veg*nism—is important to them, we cannot take away its importance simply by suggesting it isn't important. Teens often feel they are misunderstood. Now, in response to their veg*nism, you confirm that this view is accurate.

POWER. We parents are incredibly powerful, and the temptation to invoke that power whenever our children provoke our discomfort is great. No matter what feelings we may be experiencing as parents, we are the more powerful individual in relationship to a child. Parents are so powerful they may lose awareness about this immense power. Kids try a variety of ways to equalize the unequal power differential of the parent-child relationship—raising their voices, anger, and accusation. Don't lose sight of how powerful you are and how many ways you can use power against your child without even meaning to (a look, a tone of voice, a new rule, an old rule revivified, inconsistency, and unpredictability). (See also "Control.")

POWERLESSNESS. Your child may feel powerless in relation to the world, which he sees as cruel, inhumane, and inflexible. It is important to be sensitive to this sense of powerlessness as you negotiate with him how his veg*nism will be lived at home.

REJECTION. Rejection is felt on both sides of the parent-child relationship. The veg*n child often feels the parent is rejecting her and her new ethical stance. Meanwhile, as the humorist Nora Ephron suggested when she explained her child's decision to be a vegetarian, "They do it to reject you." Sometimes we take very personally our young person's efforts at exploring what it means to make decisions. Whether the issue is meat eating or something else, these decisions are often experienced as a rejection of the family. Sometimes it is seen as a reflection on a parent's imperfection. Think of it this way: our imperfections give our children solid ground to stand on! I often joke with my teenagers by saying, "Every family causes unresolved problems for the children. You are very lucky, we have given you very *interesting* unresolved problems!"

You may feel that by giving up meat, dairy, and/or eggs, your child is not only rejecting you but your family and your ethnic tradition. But your child is not rejecting your heritage, your cooking, or your love. View her veg*nism not as rejection but as one of several necessary steps to establish independence. You can help her to maintain a sense of family and ethnic connectedness by encouraging her to examine cookbooks derived from your ethnic tradition. You could challenge her to find recipes for plant-based dishes that could be contributed to your family's celebrations.

RESENTMENT. To resent a child's decision is a very painful feeling. In essence, your resentment says, "You are asking more of us than we can possibly do." It may feel like this is the case, but in fact, if you separate out the various things you are feeling, possibilities for support may become more apparent.

First, identify that you are feeling resentment. Is it from inconvenience? Frustration? What are you being asked to do that you resent?

Second, ask yourself, what—short of your child not being veg*n—can you do to stop feeling this resentment? Is there any place for middle ground? Do you need your child to assume more responsibilities in the kitchen? Tell him. Negotiate.

Third, don't ask your child to "handle" your resentment. Find ways that you can handle it: create some time for yourself; start walking; maintain your friendships. When you are feeling fulfilled in your life you may find that your feelings of resentment lessen.

RESPECT. We tend not to take teenagers seriously. An adolescent may tell her parents, "I'm in love," and her parents may say, "No you aren't." Believing a teenager about what she or he feels and believes and respects is crucial to communicating respect.

Respect is a very hard concept. People often think that the adult job is to control teenagers rather than to listen to them. Consider television's Mr. Rogers as an example of how to respect someone younger than yourself. His every action suggests that just because a child is young doesn't mean he or she is worthy of any less respect than an adult; so, too, with adolescents. Many teenagers feel warmly toward adults who treat them as adults would treat other adults, and they feel a lot of hostility toward those who treat them as adolescents.

RESPONSIBILITY. It is okay to ask your child to take responsibility for his decision. You can say, "You have to do the research. You can't just jump into it." This encourages him to develop the ability of following through on decisions that impact his own life.

RESPONSIBILITY VERSUS SELF-INTEREST. Adolescence is a time when one is learning to balance one's individual desires and needs within a new context, not that of the self, nor the family, nor the school, but of the larger world. Children who become veg*ns announce their reasons: because they don't want animals to be killed or because they are concerned about the environment or they wish to be healthy. They are acknowledging connections to a larger world and their responsibilities to that larger world. Their individual needs are being reconciled within the context of the larger world. This establishes the appropriate movement away from self and toward community. It is a valuable framework for maturity.

You might not be thrilled with their current resolution of that tension, but step back and see the achievement for what it truly is: a sign of maturity. Your child is becoming embedded within and responsible to a larger community.

SCAPEGOATING. While it is not the cause of all parent-child tensions, your child's veg*nism may become a convenient "whipping boy" for those tensions. Watch out for the temptation to blame it for all your frustrations with your child. "If only she weren't a veg*n," you may think, "then we could go to the steak house and enjoy a family meal the way we used to." You may create a notion of family harmony that never actually existed. Or you may be remembering a meal when your daughter was ten. Now that she's sixteen, she's different in so many ways and veg*nism is only one of them. You may be mistaken and think it is the veg*nism and not your child's independence that is the problem. Or perhaps you are right: you can't go to the steak house the way you used to and have a relaxed meal. But perhaps there is now something new you can do that might provide family harmony and honor your child's growth.

SELF-ESTEEM. It is difficult sometimes to have a sense of self-worth in the midsts of the changes and challenges of adolescence. Self-esteem will be buffeted by bodily changes, peer pressure, and an evolving recognition of one's relationship to the larger world. At the same time that your child's self-esteem is experiencing new and powerful stresses, it is also very important to your child's evolution: Self-esteem will influence a young person's thoughts, actions, and choices. Positive self-esteem enables experimenting, decision making, having a sense of one's potential, and envisioning a future. We parents powerfully influence our children's self-esteem. Letting our children know we respect them and trust them (through encouraging words, acknowledging an accomplishment, and listening) instills a sense of self-worth and confidence.

To reinforce their sense of self-worth by respecting the choices they make around food sends positive messages to them. Otherwise you send a message, "We might trust you in other matters, but not in this one." Be constructive rather than critical in response to your child's interests. Praise her positive traits. For instance, her veg*nism is usually motivated by admirable traits—notably, compassion. Avoid comparing your children to other children; for instance, don't complain that your child, unlike your neighbor's children, is asking too much by being veg*n.

Acknowledge her feelings; don't judge her. Trying to control her decisions sends a message that you don't trust her. No matter what the stresses your child's progress through adolescence might cause in the family and the role of veg*nism in those stresses, you can continue to affirm your child simply by saying, "I love you, I value you, I believe in you."

SHAMING TECHNIQUES. Guilt is about what you do; shame is about who you are. If you are feeling guilty you feel "I did something wrong." If you feel shamed you feel "I am wrong" or "I am bad." Saying one is ashamed of another is a virulently potent way to control someone and to destroy that person's sense of self. A person who is ashamed of herself or himself is then ashamed of every person with whom they relate.

In addition to all the standard shaming techniques of belittling, criticizing, and judging, you shame a person by telling him, when he tells you "I'm in love," or "This is very important to me," that "You're in a stage," or "This is a fad." You are saying to your child, "I have the larger vision of who you are; I know more about you than you know about yourself." Such a message is very shaming.

SPOUSAL/PARTNER TENSION. There may be tension between you and your partner over your young person's veg*nism. You may be more flexible or open to your child's interests in this area of his life than your partner is. How can you help your partner be more open to your child's interests? First, at the early stage, you may want to leave your partner out of the nitty-gritty—the examination of the contents of purchased goods, the discussions about what's for supper, the decisions about restaurants to go to. The nitty-gritty can sometimes feel frustrating, especially to someone who is not convinced of the appropriateness of this dietary change. Second, don't call attention to the food. "Look at the things Alicia can eat tonight!" or "Did you know these burgers have Portobello mushrooms in them?" Sometimes the *idea* of veg*nism is more disturbing than the reality of it. So don't keep the idea of it front and center at dinner or other times. Enjoying food often means not discussing it. Third, be relaxed yourself. Then you show, "This is easy! This can be done." Finally, understand that the nutritional rewards of this change for your child can also benefit you and your partner. Find ways to enjoy yourself as you explore veg*n foods with your young person. This may bring your partner into the joyful dynamics of eating good food, while sparing your partner some of the frustrations in living with the application of veg*nism to everyday life.

You and your partner may need to agree that the parent more involved in this aspect of life, that is, the parent who does the shopping, cooking, and kitchen maintenance, may have the lead in working with the child on this issue. This identification of role with responsibility may help to clarify lines of control and rein in the need to be absolute.

STAGES OF GROWTH. Your child's decision to make decisions about food choices should be viewed as a stage of growth that requires parenting presence as much as any other stage of growth. Now is not a time to abdicate parental interest and support but a time to interact. Your child needs opportunities to develop his individuality within the family, staying connected as he explores identity issues rather than having that aspect of his identity exiled from the home.

Responding with interest to his decision gives your young person an opportunity to develop his identity while maintaining family connectedness. (See "Acceptance.")

STARVATION. "People are starving and you aren't eating the food on the table!" Survivors of the Great Depression or a war or the Holocaust—your parents, or other immediate family members—may be shocked that a child of yours refuses food on the table. "Your relatives were starved to death. How can you pass up food?" Starvation and hunger teach an appreciation of any and all food. Is your child somehow insulting the memory of what your family experienced by not eating meat, dairy, or eggs?

It appears that way to some, and the appearance is hurtful. But you could help your older relatives see that different times require different responses to food. Their reactions are related to a certain perspective on abundance and scarcity. Your family's experience of forced scarcity has left a terrible scar. The memory of suffering associated with this is still strong. Your child is connecting to the suffering/scarcity experience and taking from it another lesson that she is applying to the reality of food inequality now. She may believe that food being fed to nonhuman animals could instead be fed directly to starving human beings. Moreover, she may not be able to articulate this clearly, but growing up in a household that remembers suffering equipped her at a deep level to be alert to the suffering of others. The difference is that these others include nonhumans. Your family can praise her process of discernment.

Your child also learned from your family's struggles around food that food is a political issue. Although she has applied the insights about the politics of food control in a way that departs from your family, she does not do so in order to dishonor the family's history. She is *extending* the gift of historical memory rather than ritualizing historical memory. As with many youth, her love looks forward; unlike many youth, her love also looks backward, too.

TEASING. The temptation to tease around food issues may be great, but so is the cost of doing so. Teasing is a subtle form of attack masked as attention. If you or other family members are teasing your child about veg*nism, you need to recognize that it is a way of controlling, embarrassing, and/or shaming him to keep him in line. Teasing does not create a motivation to change; it simply teaches your child to associate the unpleasant feeling of embarrassment with his parents or other family members. For instance, one teenager reported to me that his family insisted upon calling Gardenburgers "stinkyburgers."

Don't exploit your child's previous actions during his early childhood. It may be tempting to refer to his former vulnerabilities in an attempt to create vulnerability around his present diet. Perhaps you want to tease by saying things such as, "Remember how Allie always liked her steak at the Black Angus?" as Allie is trying to order a veg*n meal at a restaurant. Even if you feel this is a harmless comment, a mere moment of reverie recalling the child Allie was, for Allie this probably evokes several conflicting emotions: a reminder that she ate nonhuman animals: a reminder of a time when her orders at a restaurant were easy and predictable; a reminder that her parents have the power of taking her childhood apart and re-presenting it to her at awkward times.

THANKSGIVING. Your family *can* survive Thanksgiving together. Veg*n children have reported to me that this is the one day that is "absolute hell." You may feel the same thing but for different reasons. If any day seems dedicated to heightening the conflict between a veg*n and family members, it is this day. Most households cannot escape the problem: a turkey not only establishes the main course but also provides a point of departure for discussion (about how it was prepared, how it tastes, etc.). Unfortunately, the turkey is the thing that may create alienation for your child while also providing an opportunity for teasing. Relatives may say to her, "I don't know why you can't just do it this one time. It's Thanksgiving!"

Help smooth the way for your veg*n child. First, be prepared. Anticipate that your family might want to provoke an argument, using the guise of Thanksgiving tradition to criticize your child—or your parenting.

Talk with your child beforehand. Identify ways that the meal can work: "We will change the subject if someone starts to tease you, and you will reserve your comments about the meal for a time when we aren't eating." Be understanding: don't ask, "Can't we put the stuffing together?" Brainstorm a dish (or more) that can be prepared to insure there is food for your child to eat. (See recipes for Stuffed Acorn Squash and Pumpkin Cream Pie, pp. 162 and 177.)

THIRD-PERSON COMMUNICATION. Third-person communication—talking about your young person to a third person in front of your child—succeeds at signaling your frustration with your child, announcing your discomfort or inability to speak directly to your child, and thus provides a coping mechanism for you. Of course, at the same time, it belittles and embarrasses your young person, reminding him that you see him not just as a child but as childish. You might say to a friend or coworker, "My son Josh, he's a veg*n. He doesn't eat anything!" Or, "Can you imagine, Josh doesn't want to eat milk, meat, eggs! What's gotten into him?" One mother scoffed at veg*nism as an experiment and reported it derogatorily to her neighbor in front of her daughter. Her daughter told me, "That was the worst. I felt very bad."

Complaining about or criticizing your young person's actions—whether they are related to veg*nism or another aspect of her life—to your friends in your child's presence is a very hurtful act. We adults often may treat children as invisible. But that doesn't mean we are right to do so. Children are sensitive to our cues. Talking in the third person about them sends many cues: it is okay to embarrass or in other ways be unpleasant about your child in front of her when another adult is there; the adult who is present is more important than your child who is present; your child is made invisible in the presence of two adults.

Why, then, do parents resort to third-person communication? Are we using communication with the other adult to say something to our children that we are not comfortable saying directly? Are we truly so frustrated that we have to dismiss our child in front of our peers? Examine your motivations if you find yourself talking in the third person about your young person.

Another way of talking in the third person is to say at the dinner table, in front of your daughter as you are serving a meal, "Ask Julie what she is going to eat because we are going to have steak and we aren't changing." Julie may know very well you aren't changing and that you are having steak. But you are telling her something else: "You are so unimportant to me right now because of your choice not to eat meat that I cannot even acknowledge your presence." Humiliating our children because they don't agree with us is relatively easy for us. Not so easy is repairing the relationship after we have done this.

TIME-OUT. Sometimes it is okay to say, "Not now, not here. I need some time to think about this; I need some time to be alone; I need to be allowed to rest; I need to fix this food without an argument." Then you need to agree with your child to take a time-out. The essential aspect of a time-out is that neither of you must insist on having the last word and it is not done to get the upper hand. You simply have to agree to stop arguing, to allow some space—literal and figurative—to open up between you. It is hard sometimes to end an argument rather than win it. But it is up to us to initiate time-outs if we feel that the discussion is repetitious, getting too emotional, too confrontative, or if our anger—or hers—feels overwhelming.

TRUST/MISTRUST. If your response to your child's declaration of wanting to become a veg*n is "Don't be silly, of course you can't be," you are announcing mistrust. You are saying, "I can't trust you with this. It is too important." But as your child nears adulthood, the nature of the parent-child relationship should involve learning to trust your child more and more. Veg*nism is a great "practice test" for the trust relationship that you will have with your child when she is grown up. When your child becomes an adult, you will trust your child to make ethical decisions and decisions about her health. Veg*nism is a way that she is making these decisions in an environment in which her choice can be observed and supported.

Trust her to do the right thing. Help her to learn what the right thing is in terms of her health as a veg*n. And if you feel she is not eating healthily, you have not only earned her trust to be involved in solving the problem but you have also created the opportunity to help her. To be trustworthy requires that you don't lie to her, hide meat in her food, or in other ways violate her trust.

The trust you each accrue through relating to each other around these dietary changes may be laying the foundation for trust in emergencies when your teenage child is faced with a situation in which a mature, parental-type opinion is desired. Will you and your child work together to create that relationship? Or will trust be one of the missed opportunities?

ULTIMATUMS. When you feel confused or threatened by your child's behavior, you may want to fall back on that parental technique: the ultimatum. It is an attempt to bring him back in line simply through your position of greater power. You may hear yourself saying, "Absolutely not!" . . . or else "It's for your own good!" "You'll do as you are told." "Because I said so." "You're not leaving the table until you eat a piece of meat." What are you proving here? Your authority? It must be very shaky if you make ultimatums such as this.

Ultimatums are usually not successful, and if they are, it may be for the wrong reasons and offer the wrong lesson. Ultimatums teach our children that perhaps there really isn't a good reason not to be a veg*n. If there were, the reasons would be given rather than the authoritarian ultimatum.

Ultimatums help us turn our young people into some very determined adults. Often they become veg*ns at the first chance when they are out from under your control. What have those ultimatums now cost you?

The development of your child's identity will be fostered more through a democratic style of parenting than through an autocratic one that issues ultimatums. Acquiescence to your demands that he eat meat means that because its meaning for you is so great, your young person is never able to discover what meanings, if any, meat would actually have for him.

UNDERMINING. You may not acknowledge consciously that you are undermining your young person's veg*nism, but you may have taken several actions that do precisely that. Perhaps you remember a favorite meal of her childhood, say pork and beans, and decide to prepare that for an evening when everyone is together. Simultaneously, you don't actively help her prepare an alternative for her to eat. You are setting it up for her to match an emotional craving that she associates with your love and care with a physical need, to eat something for dinner. Or you might begin to fix elaborate meat meals for everyone else that look mouthwatering, while offering rice, or nothing, for your veg*n child. Or you might hide meat in her food. All of these actions are efforts at undermining your child's veg*nism. You need to examine your motivations. Why do you feel it is necessary to undermine your child? Do you believe that her decision to change her diet won't fail on the merits itself? Do you actually need to hurry it along? What concerns or frightens you about her decision?

It is sometimes hard to learn to love our children as they change, but trying to transform them back into the children they were by preparing evocative childhood favorites, or simply by being unsupportive, will not give you the child you once loved. It will create a child trapped by your need to love that old self. Her present self, this veg*n, needs your love now. But rather than encountering love your young person experiences parental undermining. Suspicion will now color the relationship between you.

If, out of love for that child she used to be, you have undermined your child, why not apologize? You can say, "I am sorry. I know how to love that old meat-eating child you used to be; I am only slowly learning how to love you as you are now. I'll try not to undermine your efforts. I want you to know I do love you."

WHAT DO YOU THINK? These are four invaluable words. We parents often are so eager to influence our children, we may say, "You probably should do X, Y, Z today, don't you think?" We *tell* them our opinions way before we hear theirs. But another way exists. Ask them, "What do you think?" We do not have to anxiously establish our children's decision-making boundaries; we can help them learn to set their own. They might say to us, "I am thinking about becoming a vegetarian." Rather than asserting an opinion—"That's a great idea."/"That's a terrible idea."—you can say, "What do you think about that?" or "Tell me what has prompted your thoughts." And then wait. Sometimes children need a little space before they can articulate what it is they are thinking and feeling.

WHY? Sometimes when we believe something very deeply, or when we are very upset, we are unable to articulate an answer when someone asks us "Why?" When unequal power relations exist, as between you and your young person, the inarticulateness becomes even more acute. You might wish that your child could clearly state all of her beliefs, could summarize her position, could answer your questions. It may not be willfulness or refusal to interact that is causing her not to answer. She simply may not be able to articulate what is going on inside her. Or she may feel embarrassed: she cares deeply about animals, so deeply it is upsetting to talk about it. She cannot find a way to bring this caring into the open to make it accessible to you. If you can, be patient and accept "Just because" as an answer and find a way to hear more than she can say.

WILL. Our most powerful force and our demon is our will. Our child's growth to adulthood is going to come in conflict with our will. Our will then prompts an inner dialogue, such as "Who do they think they are?" or "Why aren't they listening to me?" We want things our way. No matter what models we have had in the past, parenting is not, actually, a dictatorship. And we have not been successful parents just because our will prevails.

WORRY. It seems as though it is the nature of parenting to worry about our children. The challenge is to determine which worries are legitimate and need to be addressed and which worries are overinflated and need to be dismissed. Your child's health, nutritional needs, and growth are all major concerns when a change in diet occurs. But worries that arise about veg*nism can be reframed. That is why, for instance, we have placed information on anemia under the entry on "Iron-rich Foods," and information on osteoporosis under "Bone Health" in chapter 3. Reassure yourself that you are being a good parent in supporting your child's veg*nism, because, in fact, you are.

2

Practical Issues

When my son Ben was a toddler, his absolutely favorite book was *A, B, C, D, Tummy, Toes, Hands, Knees*. In graceful watercolors, the story depicts a day in the life of one loving mother and one active toddler. The "Mom" in the story feeds her toddler breakfast in the kitchen. Then they gather their stuff together and head out the door. One catches a glimpse of fresh fruit on the otherwise clean dining room table. Child happily in stroller, they walk to town. Mom mails a letter, together they shop in a grocery store, return a book to the library, and then they head to the park for a picnic. The child gets thoroughly dirty. The adventure over, they arrive back home, the Mom gives the child a bath with happy, messy splashing, and then it is off to bed.

I was a very tired mom at that time in Ben's life, trying to meet some writing deadlines while also being present to him in his early years. Each day that I read that book to him, all I could think about was how much work the mother had done to create those experiences: She had fixed breakfast and cleaned up, she had fixed a picnic lunch and gotten it packed up, she had had time to write a letter, and to return books to the library; she had time to supervise her child's bath. Each time I read the book I felt more tired from the sheer reminder of the demands, often unrecognized, of rearing a child.

You might feel the same thing about your child's decision to be a veg*n. You *want* to support him or her, but, gee, it's no picnic. Someone has to fix breakfast *and* lunch *and* dinner; someone has to clean up from breakfast *and* lunch *and* dinner. And there are other practical concerns: If your child has become a vegan, what soaps for a bath are available that have no animal products in them? How will planning for celebrations and holidays, much less picnics, be affected by this dietary change?

The practical aspects of supporting your child might feel overwhelming. It feels like your child's change of diet requires not just an overhaul of your mind but of your pantry and perhaps of your cooking style. Don't despair. Think about the practical issues in metaphoric terms: you are simply walking alongside your child on this path. You aren't pushing her (and not just because she no longer fits into a stroller), and though at times it feels like you are lagging behind her when it comes to food preparation, meal planning, and nutrition, you feel intimately involved. Think of veg*nism as a journey you can accompany her on. You can ask your child, "What are you learning about vegetable protein?" Your local grocery store, especially if it is part of a chain, has already begun to stock more vegetarian and vegan items. Soymilk is often available in both the refrigerator section and a "natural foods" section of most supermarkets. Many frozen food sections now have a "vegetarian" or "organic" section of a freezer with veggie burgers, and vegetarian and vegan frozen dinners. You can go together to your local store and see what it already has. You might take the Pantry List found on pp. 75–77 and check it against what the grocery store currently has in stock. Consider requesting items that they don't carry, for instance, Vegenaise, a terrific mayonnaise substitute, or Tofutti products.

As with any journey, take this one step by step, product by product.

You can ask for a tour of a natural foods store. You are exploring together. Walking alongside your child helps to reduce awkward power dynamics that sometimes trip us up; you are learning together.

But it's time-consuming. Yes, this is true. Like any major change in the family (like joining the band!), a veg*n in the family will seem time-consuming.

But take a moment and think about "time." Remember that child who hung around the kitchen and talked to you after school? Or wanted to go for a walk or play a game with you? Or even the child who rode in a stroller? That child has disappeared, and now there is a different child in your life, one who is very busy, very involved in life with other youth, perhaps rarely home (see "Nomad Year" in chapter 1). The one thing you want and need with your young person—"quality time"—is suddenly offered to you but in a very unexpected package: veg*nism. Planning a menu, creating a shopping list, shopping, preparing a new recipe together, and then enjoying the fruits of your efforts as you eat together—

these are all opportunities to spend time with your young person. You may not welcome it, it may seem time-consuming and frustrating, but this truly is a gift. Not only does it give you time with your child, it prepares him for knowing how to fix good food once on his own as well as giving him a terrific memory of a special time with a parent.

Again, it is a step-by-step process. You might begin with the question that presents itself every day: What shall we have for supper? Recipes, many easy, using predictable, easily obtained ingredients can be found in chapter 5. But don't stop there. Consider recipes that move you, step by step, into some of the delightful areas of meatless cooking. In the recipe section you will encounter "steddas." These are *instead of* . . . for instance "stedda feta," or "stedda sour cream." These provide nondairy standbys for a veg*n kitchen. Usually simple to make, steddas can help a child have some standard foods to eat. (See also "Substitutes" in this chapter.)

If you have always cooked for your child, don't stop now.

But yes, negotiate chores. Expand your repertoire *and* your negotiating skills. Supporting your child through awareness of the practical issues that veg*nism presents helps your child feel more confident and loved; and, as with any walk, even ones that simply take us to town and back, there are surprises along the way for us, too.

BAR OR BAT MITZVAHS. If a child becomes a vegetarian at eleven or twelve, this issue might manifest and express itself during the year that your child is preparing for her bat mitzvah or his bar mitzvah. Two issues may present themselves: first, the issue of the choice of food for the Kiddish luncheon or an evening party (see "Parties" and "Celebrations"). Second, their mitzvah project might be related to this issue. Usually the rabbi wants the mitzvah project to express an interest of the child. Mitzvah projects with veg*n themes include: working at an animal shelter; conducting a campaign for donations of food, blankets, and other supplies for a shelter; organizing a vegetarian meal at a homeless shelter; or creating an environmental project related to meat eating and vegetarianism. Encourage them to research the possibilities and discuss the ideas with your rabbi.

BIRTHDAYS. (See also "Celebrations.") Just because someone is a veg*n should not prevent a delicious cake from being consumed. Birthday cakes are ways of saying "You are special." "We want to celebrate the unique individual you are!" You can order a cake or make one, but be sure to have one if cakes have always been a part of your birthday celebrations.

In our household, one son loves to celebrate his birthday with a nondairy cheesecake from Delicious Choices. You can order them from www.deliciouschoices.com or 1-402-420-1320. Sticky Fingers Bakery also makes delicious baked goods, www.stickyfingersbakery .com or 1-202-299-9700. You can also make a vegan birthday cake (for recipes see pp. 170–77).

BOOKS. At some point your child may ask you to read a book—or ten—on the subject of veg*nism. She may implore you to do so. You may not trust the book's point of view, facts, or author simply because your child has thrust it upon you. Remind yourself of the tuba principle: you do not have to study music or learn to play the tuba in order to support your child's interest in the instrument. You do not need to do so now. Whereas your child feels very deeply about this, and although there are many good books on the subject, most people do not enjoy being forced to read anything. You are probably the same way. This book in your hands may be the compromise. You might meet her here. If, after using this book, you feel you can be open to another one, you might start with vegan cookbooks or ask your child to narrow her request to one article.

BREAKFAST POSSIBILITIES. In addition to the recipes listed for "Breakfasts" in chapter 5, other breakfast possibilities include: bagel with peanut butter, oatmeal, muffins, leftover pizza, leftover rice and veggies, soy yogurt, fruit salad, cereal plus nuts plus dried fruits.

CANDLES. Most candles contain animal products. You can obtain vegetable-based candles from different sources, including some of the vegan catalogs. They can also be ordered from the Riverbend Candle Company, 1-309-788-6380. (See "Vegan Products.")

CELEBRATIONS. Celebrations, like birthdays, generally recognize a vital moment in the life of an individual, a couple, or a community. Some celebrations often mark a passage from one stage to another: from child to adult (graduations and bar and bat mitzvahs), or from being single to getting married. Celebrations also affirm relationships among individuals, families, or communities. Food is generally an essential component of most celebrations. If the celebration centers on your veg*n child's accomplishments, birthday, graduation, bar or bat mitzvah, wedding, etc., and that veg*n child wants the celebration to be veg*n, what should you do?

Well, why not honor this basic desire? Since you are balancing your child's needs with your own expectations and what tradition requires, you may think, "This celebration needs to have meat." Everyone else except your vegan child may believe this, too. But a creative solution exists that can honor your child's desire and the need to provide foods that celebrate the occasion: agree to provide veg*n food, but don't make a big deal about it with your guests.

If the food is good—and of course it can be—your guests will not even realize there is anything to make a fuss about. They really won't miss the meat. They will also take their cue from you. If you are relaxed about this decision, you will communicate this ease to others.

Celebrations are about inclusion not exclusion, and if your child's accomplishments are central to the celebrations, let his or her veg*nism be expressed through the celebration. (See also "Parties.")

CHOCOLATE. Your young person may have given up dairy and eggs but not necessarily chocolate. Recipes for chocolate treats can be found on pages 170–76. Many companies also offer vegan chocolate treats. Dairy-free chocolate in a variety of flavors and shapes (for different holidays) is available from Chocolate Decadence at www.chocolatedecadence.com or 1-800-324-5018. Simple Treats provides mail-order chocolate chips, brownies, and blondies (Simple Treats, Main Street Mercantile, #9, Eastham, MA 02642, www.simpletreats.com or 1-508-255-6244). Wax Orchards features a variety of fudges (22744 Wax Orchards Road, Vashon Island, WA 98070; www.waxorchards.com or 1-800-634-6132). Delicious Choices provides dairy-free cheesecakes. (See "Birthdays.")

CHORES. Vegetarianism, rather than being a burden on the household's food preparer, can be an opportunity to empower your child. After all, children will need to learn to shop and cook eventually anyway. Your goal should be to empower them in a loving way, to invite them into the wonderful process of creating in the kitchen. How do you do this? Involve them in all aspects of meal preparation—planning, shopping, cooking, and cleaning up. Sit down with them to make up a shopping list. Go shopping together. Offer to cook with them. Suggest they cook a meal for the family. Create a chart that makes responsibilities clear.

COLLEGES/UNIVERSITIES. It is estimated that at least fifteen percent of the nation's fifteen million college students eat vegetarian meals. Colleges and universities across the country are responding to the veg*n needs of this group of students. If your high school student is looking at colleges, you should feel comfortable inquiring about veg*n entrees at meals. One school we visited proudly boasted to all parents that they had one of the top vegan cafeterias according to People for the Ethical Treatment of Animals. PETA and Vegan Action provide suggestions for college students on how to veganize their cafeteria (CollegeAction@PETA-online.org or call 1-757-622-7382, and www.vegan.org/campaigns/dorm_food/index.html). Physicians Committee for Responsible Medicine offers dining services a "Gold Plan," a no-cholesterol, low-fat, animal-free nutrition plan designed especially for institutions. PCRM can be contacted at pcrm@pcrm.org or 1-202-686-2210.

In addition, *The Teen's Vegetarian Cookbook* has a section on "College Cuisine." Finally, the Vegetarian Resource Group provides information for students at non-vegetarian-friendly campuses on how to insure healthy balanced meals for themselves (www.vrg.org/).

COMFORT FOODS. Comfort foods are the foods you make that say "I love you." Your child still needs comfort foods, and you may also feel a need to provide food that comforts—it is both a symbolic and literal form of nurturing. Some of the old traditional comfort foods are now "tainted," but alternative veg*n comfort foods can be made, from hot chocolate (made with soymilk) to tomato soup (Imagine Brand makes a vegan tomato soup that you can combine with equal amounts of soymilk, add a little oregano and pepper, and instant comfort!). I have included recipes for Comforting Pot Pie (p. 151), Orzo Pilaf (p. 161), Scalloped Potatoes (p. 169), Ginger Peachy Bread Pudding (p. 175), "Cottage Cheese" (p. 140).

CONVENIENCE FOODS. Many canned and frozen foods can be used in making a veg*n meal: spaghetti sauce without meat, canned soups, canned vegetarian baked beans, refried beans without lard, and veggie burgers, to name a few. Several vegan cookbooks jump to the task of providing reliable recipes for quick meals: Debra Wasserman's *Conveniently Vegan: Turn Packaged Foods into Delicious Vegetarian Dishes* offers recipes as well as a very helpful appendix that lists sources of vegan products. Also extremely useful are Virginia Messina and Kate Schumann's *The Convenient Vegetarian: Quick-and-Easy Meatless Cooking* and Polly Pitchford and Delia Quigley's *Cookin' Healthy With One Foot Out the Door: Quick Meals for Fast Times.*

COOKBOOKS. A wonderful abundance of good veg*n cookbooks that provide tasty meals for veg*ns and nonveg*ns alike are now available.

Several are aimed at the teen crowd, among them *The Teen's Vegetarian Cookbook* by Judy Krizmanic and Matthew Wawiorka and *Munchie Madness: Vegetarian Meals for Teens* by Dorothy R. Bates, Bobbie Hinman, Robert Oser, and Suzanne Havala. Many veg*n teens I have met love Myra Kornfield's *The Voluptuous Vegan*—she provides incredible recipes that truly take vegan cooking to a new level. Canadians Tanya Barnard and Sarah Kramer's *How It All Vegan* and *The Garden of Vegan* have been wildly successful with young people.

For all-around balance, taste, and trustworthy recipes, Jennifer Raymond's *The Peaceful Palate* is superb. Any cookbooks by "uncheese" pioneer Joanne Stepaniak are bound to please many in your family, not only your veg*n; her *Vegan Vittles* is a good introduction to her creative way of cooking. Dreena Burton's *The Everyday Vegan: Recipes and Lessons for Living the Vegan Life* is extremely helpful. Beverly Lynn Bennett, "The Vegan Chef," offers her *Eat Your Veggies! Recipes from the Kitchen of the Vegan Chef* as a downloadable PDF file at www.veganchef.com. Ken Haedrich's *Feeding the Healthy Vegetarian Family* is a thoughtful and reliable addition to the field of cookbooks. And don't miss Robin Robertson's *The Vegetarian Meat and Potatoes Cookbook*; it's fantastic.

Finally, two great cookbooks are aimed at those who want to bake without animal products. Superlatives abound when baking from Meredith McCarty's *Sweet and Natural: More than 120 Sugar-Free and Dairy-Free Desserts.* Fran Costigan's cover says it all for her marvelous cookbook, *Great Good Desserts Naturally! Secrets of Sensational Sin-Free Sweets*: "No Milk. No Butter. No Eggs. Zero Cholesterol. Refined Sugar-Free. No Junk. No Hard Work. No Kidding. You won't believe these are healthy desserts." (See also the cookbooks listed at "Convenience Foods.")

COOKING. If you have always prepared meals for your child, don't stop cooking for her if you continue to cook for the others in the household. This could send a message of rejection to your child. Identify ways that your food can include a veg*n component. Ask your child to help you develop a menu of foods your whole family can embrace. This time is a wonderful opportunity to involve your child in kitchen responsibilities. It equips her for life on her own. Offer to teach her how to cook veg*n things that you know how to cook; offer to cook with her; offer to learn how to cook new things as long as she learns alongside with you.

Cooking with your child or young person may be a surprising opportunity for fun, for talking, for relaxing together. As the focus becomes preparing good-tasting foods, disagreements may melt away. Being together in this way may be one of the memorable events you will recall when your young person has left home for college or work. I know this is true for me: my two teenage boys have labored with me to make time-consuming but delicious homemade ravioli—we have made two fillings as well as the pasta for the ravioli shell. We have been silly and we have been silent. They loved to eat the food they prepared. Even when they were younger, they were helping squeeze out the spinach for spanakopita and handling the phyllo dough. And they have good memories of the experience, too.

EATING OUT. When eating out, advance preparation is everything for a veg*n. You and your child should not assume anything about the waitstaff (i.e., that they know what "vegetarian" means, that they understand this means not eating foods made with chicken stock, that they know "Parmesan" means cheese, that they understand that gelatin, lard, and anchovies are animal products). This is one reason to do as much negotiating with the restaurant on behalf of your veg*n's needs before arriving there. You can also suggest restaurants that serve food of a vegetarian nature. Thai, Ethiopian, Chinese, and Indian restaurants usually offer vegetarian entrees. At a pizzeria, your child can order a cheeseless pizza with vegetables and a little olive oil drizzled on top.

If your child knows in advance what restaurant is planned on, she can check out the Internet for restaurant reviews by the local paper or for the restaurant's Web site. If you have a fax machine, she can have a menu faxed to her. She can call and talk to the chef or kitchen manager (but not at the height of mealtimes!). Ken Haedrich, winner of the Julia Child Cookbook Award, explains, "He or she should be willing and able to talk to you intelligently about the sort of food you would like. And you should get the distinct impression that the chef knows something about meatless cuisine and looks at feeding you as a creative challenge, not as a pain." You might begin by asking, "What vegetarian entrees do you offer?" This lets them know that at least one person assumes they should be offering veg-etarian entrees.

Specific questions that can be asked include: Do you put chicken stock in soups or sauces (such as tomato sauces or other sauces that go over pasta)? Are there eggs in your pasta? What do you cook your french fries in? (Not, Do you cook your french fries in vegetable oil or animal fat?) Do you cook your tomato sauce with meat and then strain it out? Does the chef use a meat-based stock for flavoring or thinning?

If there are no vegetarian entrees, perhaps your veg*n can try to determine if a meat meal can be prepared without the meat: A Porto-bello mushroom and meat sandwich could have the meat left out; A reuben sandwich with sauerkraut and avocado can be pretty tasty. Pasta with steamed, roasted, or grilled vegetables in an olive oil-garlic sauce is good. A set of side dishes and/or appetizers can be combined into a vegetable plate.

EAT YOUR VEGGIES! Use this as an opportunity to introduce your young person to foods you have always wanted him to eat. One teenager said to me, "Parents are always complaining that their kids aren't eating vegetables, and then when they only eat vegetables, they get upset." Now you can say, "Look, a broccoli (chard, kale, spinach) casserole!" and they may well be thrilled.

FAST FOOD. Traditional fast food has been heavily marketed to young people. It appears that one of the appeals of hamburgers is that small hands can hold them. So, too, with Chicken McNuggets. Burger King and McDonald's have put out the welcome mat to families with their play areas. Fast food is convenient for the hurried family. If fast food is a food of choice for your family, your veg*n may still be able to get food at various fast food places. The Vegetarian Resource Group sur-veyed over 100 fast-food, casual and family-style restaurant chains, and has published the results in their *Guide to Fast Food: Vegetarian Menu Items at Restaurants and Quick Service Chains.* You can find information on it at www.vrg.org or by calling 1-410-366-8343.

Veg*n cooking is not necessarily time-consuming. At home your veg*n child can have veggie burgers with ketchup/mustard/relish (or nonmeat gravy or barbecue sauce), "not" dogs with vegetarian baked beans, Ramen noodles, or store-bought pizza crusts. (See "Convenience Foods" for a list of veg*n recipes for harried cooks.)

From veg*n baking mixes to instant macaroni-and-cheese packages, many products exist for quick preparation of veg*n food. They can be ordered from places like Dixie Diner or Pangea. (See "Vegan Products" for contact information.)

FAUX MEATS: Vegetable protein in the shape of or with the taste of meat includes frozen ground "beef," frozen ground "sausage," veggie hot dogs, veggie burgers, veggie deli slices, and "tofurky." Many faux meats can be found at your local supermarket (often in the vegetable or frozen food section). They can also be ordered from catalogs and online companies. (See "Vegan Products" for contact information.)

FILM. Digital cameras solve the problem that camera film isn't vegan.

GIFTS. Respect your child's decision and don't give her products that are inconsistent with her veg*nism. If she is a vegan, avoid gifts of wool, silk, leather, fur, or milk chocolate. Show her you can respect her decision. Check out "Vegan/Vegetarian Resources" for a wide variety of gifts for your young person, from clothing, shoes, and boots, to foods.

HIDDEN INGREDIENTS. If your child has decided to become a veg*n, you may be asking yourself, Why do what seem like infinitesimal amounts of animal products matter? Why can't veg*ns eat bread with whey in it, nondairy cheese with casein or honey? Why *can't* they pick out the meat? Because your child has decided that animal products represent something he objects to—be it cruelty to animals or environmental degradation. The entire food item is contaminated by the presence of that which is seen as unethical or unenvironmental. Recently McDonald's was sued because they used beef flavor in their french fries, french fries they had guaranteed were vegetarian. At first, they seemed to argue, "What's an infinitesimal amount of beef flavor?" But they soon realized there is no such thing as "infinitesimal." To veg*ns, there are veg*n foods and there are non-veg*n foods. There is no in-between. And McDonald's, realizing their culpability, settled the suit, offered public apologies, and removed beef flavor from the french fries.

You may feel uncomfortable as your child interrogates a waitperson about the contents of a tomato sauce or soup, or as she examines the contents of a salad dressing at the grocery store. The way to honor this attempt to live a life with integrity is to find a way for you to be patient with her. Take a deep breath. Remind yourself that she is becoming an educated consumer. Allow yourself to be surprised when you realize how many different items contain animal products.

If we are supporting our young people in their veg*nism, we cannot try to dissuade them from food items simply because "there is only a little meat in it." The amount doesn't matter; the principle does. So, please don't hide meat in a meal you are preparing. You may be concerned that your child needs some nutrient in meat, and you decide to make sure he gets it by hiding meat in the food you prepare for him. *But all you teach your child is that you are not to be trusted.* At times when you feel anxious for him, remind yourself that no matter how alien it is to you, this change in diet will not harm your child.

Hidden ingredients to watch out for include:

- In prepared soups, stocks, and sauces: chicken or beef stock, lard, gelatin
- In baked goods, pastas, puddings, and candy bars: whey, eggs, cow's milk, albumin, suet
- In nondairy cheeses: casein
- In beans and tortillas: lard
- In candies: gelatin in Gummi Bears, Altoids, and marshmallows; lard in chewing gum
- In salad dressings: cow's milk, sour cream, yogurt, cheese, gelatin.

Vegetarian Journal's Guide to Food Ingredients provides assistance in determining what foods have been, in the view of your veg*n, rendered contaminated because they contain animal products. Joanne Stepaniak's chapter "Secret Ingredients" in her book *The Vegan Sourcebook* also is helpful.

HOLIDAYS. Affirm that celebrations around food are about people gathered together and not what is on the plate (even if up until now that was not necessarily true). Include your young person in menu planning. Review the ground rules for eating together. (See also "Thanksgiving.")

KITCHEN EQUIPMENT. To insure that your child is eating healthy veg*n meals, you might consider getting for your kitchen:

A nonstick electric skillet—the perfect solution to several potential or actual kitchen concerns. Your child will have a cooking surface that has not been contaminated by animal products (a concern for many young veg*ns). Food may be prepared for your young person's meal while the dinner meal is being prepared for everyone else, without needed space on the stovetop being usurped. Its size allows one pound of sliced or cubed tofu to be cooked at a time. Your child can take the skillet with him when he moves out. It is great for making scrambled tofu and pancakes.

A blender—for making smoothies, tofu ricotta, spreads, grinding flax-seeds to use as egg substitutes, and soups.

A rice steamer—to insure that your child will have a basic staple available. Steamers are inexpensive and can be used to steam vegetables, too. The best thing about them is that they require no attention once the rice and the water have been added. Brown rice cooked earlier in the day can quickly be made into stir-fried rice with vegetables for supper, rice salad or rice pudding.

A cutting board—because salmonella is only destroyed at high temperatures. If a veg*n uses the same cutting board to cut up salad ingredients as one that has been used to cut up chicken, the veg*n food may be contaminated with salmonella that will not be destroyed by cooking. For this reason, a cutting board should be acquired that is dedicated solely to veg*n food preparation.

Immersion Blender—a wandlike, mobile, versatile, and powerful blender. Unlike traditional blenders in which you transfer the food into the blender, with the cordless model immersion blender you bring *it* to your food. It can blend or puree in the bowl or pan in which the ingredients already are being prepared. By reducing the number of steps in food preparation, it is a valuable time-saver.

A soymilk maker—because homemade soymilk is delicious and inexpensive. The Vancouver Island Vegetarian Association (www.Island Veg.com) did a product review of soymilk machines, which they published in the Winter 2003 issue of *The Veggie Platter*. They recommend the Soylife Soymilk Maker, calling it "the clear winner." For information on this machine see www.ezsoymilk.com or 1-888-769-5433.

A pressure cooker—while a pressure cooker is more of a financial investment than some other kitchen utensils, it is a true time-saver. As the subtitle to one cookbook announces, "Two-hour taste in ten minutes." A pressure cooker can prepare soups, stews, casseroles, vegetables, grains, beans, and desserts. (The title of the book is *Great Vegetarian Cooking Under Pressure*, by Lorna Sass.)

KITCHEN PANTRY. See "Pantry List."

LEATHER. Why won't your veg*n child wear leather anymore? Leather is a byproduct of the slaughtering process; it is made frequently from "spent" dairy cows. If your child is a vegan, she objects to any product that derives from the killing of animals. Furthermore, many meat eaters taunt vegetarians by saying, "If you are a vegetarian, why are you wearing leather?" Those meat eaters recognize that consistency is an important aspect of following an ethical path. This is what your child is trying to do. Wallets, shoes, boots, purses, and coats are now available in nonleather material. Check out the Internet sources listed under "Web sites" for examples of these products. The Vegetarian Resource Group provides information on leather alternatives at www.vrg.org/nutshell/leather.htm.

MAKING DEALS. If you are willing to cook for your veg*n child, don't continually protest or complain about how much work it is. Instead, make deals: "I will do this, if you can agree to this. . . ." Use the opportunity to support your child in something important to her, but have her help you with something important to you.

MEAL PLANNING. Meal planning may help make your child's transition to veg*nism easier, especially for the one who is responsible for preparing meals. It can begin the process of involving your child in cooking. Ask your child to help identify possible meals for the coming week. It can reduce the stress at the end of a hectic day. The question of "What are we going to eat?" has already been anticipated and answered. Plan a week's worth of menus at a time. Identify how your regular meals can be veganized (stir-fries, or pasta with marinara sauce, for instance). Together, identify a night when your child could cook for the entire family.

PANTRY LIST. This is a basic pantry list to get you started with vegetarian cooking. You may not wish to use all of these items. Some families won't cook with curry powder, for example, or use sea vegetables. If some of these foods are not familiar, start with a few from each category and experiment to find out which ones appeal to your vegetarian child.

GRAINS

Barley
Bulgur
Cornmeal
Couscous
Millet
Popcorn
Quinoa
Rice, brown
Rolled oats, quick oats, and/or
    instant oatmeal
Wheat berries
Wheat germ

Italian pasta (macaroni,
    spaghetti, etc.)
Asian pasta (mung-bean
    noodles, soba noodles,
    Ramen noodles, udon)
Ready-to-eat cereal
Flour, whole wheat and/or
    enriched white

BREADS

Graham crackers
Pita
Rice cakes
Tortillas, flour and corn
Whole grain crackers
Whole wheat bagels and
    English muffins

DRIED BEANS

Black beans, black-eyed peas,
    chickpeas or garbanzos,
    great northern, kidney,
    lentils, limas, navy, pinto,
    soybeans, split peas

FRUITS AND VEGETABLES

Any variety of fresh, canned,
    or frozen
Dried fruits (applies, apricots,
    currants, dates, figs, papaya,
    peaches, raisins)
Dried sea vegetables (alaria,
    arame, dulse, hijiki,
    kombu, nori, and wakame)
Garlic and onions

SOY PRODUCTS

Faux meats (veggie burgers,
    hot dogs, sausage, etc.)
Soy cheese and yogurt
Tempeh
Textured vegetable protein
Tofu

CANNED BEANS AND VEGETABLES

Beans: vegetarian baked
    beans, black beans, chili
    beans, garbanzos, kidney,
    limas, pinto

Spaghetti sauce
Tomato products: diced,
  stewed, sauce, paste
Vegetables

PREPARED FOODS

Chili
Hummus
Instant dried bean mixes
  (black beans, refried beans)
Polenta
Salad dressings
Soups
Tofu scrambler mix
Tofu spread

NUTS AND SEEDS

Almonds, cashews, hazelnuts,
  peanuts, pecans, pine nuts,
  walnuts
Nut and seed butters (almond,
  cashew, peanut, sesame seed
  tahini)
Pumpkin, sesame, sunflower
  seeds

BEVERAGES

Fortified soymilk
Fruit and vegetable juices

CONDIMENTS

Barbecue sauce
Blackstrap molasses
Coconut milk

Curry pastes
Dried herbs and spices
Hot pepper sauce
Jams and preserves
Kelp powder
Ketchup
Mayonnaise
Miso
Mustard
Olives
Pickles
Relish
Salsa
Sun-dried tomatoes in oil
Tamari soy sauce
Thai peanut sauce
Vegetable broth powder
Vegetarian Support Formula
  Nutritional Yeast
Vinegar (apple cider,
  balsamic, herb-infused,
  rice)
Worcestershire sauce
  (low-sodium type is
  vegetarian)

FATS

Canola oil
Flaxseed oil
Ground flaxseed
Olive oil
Soy oil

PARTIES. If your child is hosting a party for his peers, many foods are available for veg*n treats. Pasta dishes are always successful entrees. You can get a six-foot-long submarine sandwich roll and heap it with veggies, faux meats ("salami," "tofurky"), sprouts, olives, and pickles. If the party is to be a fancy one, many local caterers are very creative and can, when presented with a veg*n cookbook, discover something they can prepare if they haven't already faced that challenge.

RESEARCH. Help your teen research information on veg*nism the way you would help her research a college. What nutrients does she need? What basic foods are available? What foods are already consumed in your household? What small adjustments could be made to accommodate her? The next chapter will answer all the basic nutritional questions that a vegetarian diet raises.

RESTAURANTS. See "Eating Out."

SEVEN BASIC MEALS. The average family eats seven regular dinner meals. Many of these can be adapted to a veg*n diet with little stress. Identify your household's seven basic meals. Which ones are already vegetarian? Baked potatoes? Soups? Macaroni and cheese? Which ones can become vegetarian? What substitutions can easily be made? Can spaghetti and meatballs become spaghetti in a mushroom sauce, spaghetti with tofu balls, spaghetti with texturized soy protein?

You can develop new recipes using favorite veg*n food as a base. For instance, if the perennial family favorite is pasta, you can make spaghetti primavera, spaghetti marinara, or Asian noodles. You can make grilled pizzas, veggie pizzas, or pesto pizzas. You can create mix-and-match meals. Make your own burritos, with choices of lettuce, salsa, tomatoes, mushrooms, sun-dried tomatoes, and tofu or texturized soy protein for your veg*n. You can go ethnic. Many cuisines use meat as a condiment rather than as a main course. Select dishes that could have meat added to them if the diners so desired (such as stir-fries, curries, and Middle Eastern platters).

SHOES. Many places sell nonleather shoes. Surprisingly, a major source is the chain Payless Shoe Source. But your child may object to buying shoes from China or other places where it is evident that sweatshop standards prevail in the making of products for the American market. If that is the case, you can help your son or daughter find nonleather shoes at speciality places such as:

- ᓀ MooShoes, 207 East 26th Street, New York, NY 10010 (1-212-481-5792) and on the Web at www.mooshoes.com
- ᓀ Heartland Products (they make great cowboy boots!): 1-515-332-3089; www.trvnet.net~hrtlndp

Besides the stores that specialize in nonleather shoes, the major veg*n Web sites also offer a wide variety of shoes: Pangea, Vegan Essentials, and TheVegetarianSite.com. (See "Vegan Vegetarian Products.")

SHOPPING LIST. With your child, you can plan a full week of menus. Identify what you plan to cook and brainstorm with your veg*n child what he or she could have. If you are adventurous, explore the possibilities of other cultures' plant-based foods. If you are more conservative, help your child identify meals that are adaptations of your planned meals. Make a shopping list based on the coexisting meal plans that you develop. A basic veg*n shopping list can be created by looking at the Pantry List (see pp. 75–77).

SNACKS: Veg*n snacks can include: muffins, soymilk and cookies, popcorn with nutritional yeast sprinkled on it, fruits plus Tofu "Cottage Cheese" (see p. 140), rice cakes with peanut butter/almond butter/ cashew butter, hot chocolate with soy- or rice milk, tortilla chips with Nacho Sauce (see p. 139), frozen bananas (peeled, rolled in carob powder and nuts, then frozen); "ants on a log"—celery stalks spread with peanut butter and decorated with raisins, pretzels, salsa, and instant black beans.

SOAPS. Many commercial soaps use animal products. If your child is a vegan, these soaps will now be objectionable. But many sources for plant-based soaps exist. Tom's of Maine makes natural glycerin soaps free of animal products. Dr. Bronner's and Kirk's also make such soaps and should be widely available. If you have Asian or Indian stores nearby, many Indian soaps are made from pure vegetable ingredients. You can also order soaps from North American Naturals, 19 Cheshire Road, Allendale Plaza, Pittsfield, MA, 01201, 1-877-833-SOAP, or www.nansoap.com or www.vegsoap.com.

STEDDAS. "Steddas," as noted, are *instead of.* They are foods that you can prepare as substitutes for traditional and popular products such as sour cream and eggs. See the recipe section for some basic stedda recipes (pp. 137–40).

SUBSTITUTES. Some basic substitution in food preparation is necessary. Here are some of the more common substitutions necessary to prepare a veg*n dish:

- Chicken, beef, veal, or other animal-based stock: Use vegetable broth. Options include Imagine's Organic No-Chicken Broth or Pacific's Mushroom Broth (in 32-ounce boxes); Take Stock's frozen vegetable stock; or "chicken-flavored" vegetarian stock powder.
- Worcestershire sauce (it contains anchovies): Vegetarian Worcestershire sauce or substitute soy sauce with a dash of apple cider vinegar.
- Bacon bits (for salads, etc.): Use a vegetarian alternative or set some salad aside.
- Bottled tomato sauce with meat: Use marinara sauces, but check the label; for vegans, avoid those with Parmesan cheese, butter, whey, or cream.
- Substitute "faux meats" in sloppy joes, tacos, tomato sauce, and chili.
- Mashed potatoes: Sometimes potatoes are cooked in chicken broth. Try cooking some of them in No-Chicken Broth instead.
- Eggs: For baked goods, substitute ¼ cup silken tofu per egg, or ¼ cup mashed banana per egg. If only one egg is needed, omit the egg and replace with 2 tablespoons of liquid, 2 tablespoons cornstarch or arrowroot or potato starch. Flaxseeds provide a wonderful substitute: 1 tablespoon flaxseeds, finely ground up in a blender then mixed with 3 tablespoons of water, will produce the equivalent of one egg. Ener-G Egg Replacer is a commercial product you can use. Depending on the flavors in your dish, you could choose one of the following to thicken casseroles: cornstarch, potato starch, arrowroot

powder, mashed potatoes, tahini, peanut or other nut butters, or tomato paste.

- Butter: A nondairy margarine, such as Earth Balance Natural Buttery Spread, Spectrum Naturals Organic Margarine, or Canoleo Soft Margarine.

- Milk: Soymilk, rice milk, and nut milks. Soymilks are now available in most grocery stores.

- Buttermilk: For 1 cup of buttermilk place 1 tablespoon of apple cider vinegar or lemon juice in a 1-cup measuring cup, then fill with soymilk. Let stand for a few minutes.

- Sour cream: Tofutti Sour Supreme "Better than Sour Cream" or make your own using silken tofu mixed with a little lemon juice and salt (see recipe on p. 140).

- Yogurt: Use plain soy yogurt.

- Honey: Brown rice syrup, Fruitsource, or maple syrup.

- Cream: White Wave's Silk Soymilk Creamer.

- Cream cheese: Tofutti Better than Cream Cheese.

- Mayonnaise: Several vegan mayonnaises are available. My favorite is Follow Your Heart's Vegenaise.

- Cheese: Soymage vegan cheese; but don't expect vegan cheeses to perform in the same way as dairy cheeses. Nutritional yeast has a cheesy flavor. A wonderful cookbook by Joanne Stepaniak, *The Uncheese Cookbook*, provides recipes for cheese substitutes using nutritional yeast. Try the Nacho Sauce on page 139 and see for yourself how yummy a cheese sauce can be made from nutritional yeast.

- Vegetable gratins can be made without eggs, milk, or cheese.

- For recipes that call for sautéing vegetables in butter, sauté them in a combination of olive oil and vegan margarine, or simply with olive oil.

- Salad dressing: Either avoid dressings with honey, mayonnaise, Parmesan cheese, milk, or buttermilk, or leave a part of your salad untossed with dressing. See pages 138, 163, and 165 for salad dressing recipes.

- Before mashing potatoes, set some aside and use plain soymilk and margarine.

- Ice cream: Many sorbets are dairy-free (including Häagen-Daz's and Marble Slab's) and nondairy frozen desserts abound! Your grocery store may carry Soy Delicious, Tofutti, and/or Rice Dream frozen products.

🍃 White sugar: Sucanat, maple sugar, or concentrated fruit sweeteners (can be ordered from Wax Orchards).

TOFU-PHOBIA. You or someone you love may be a tofu-phobe—having an irrational fear of tofu. Yet your veg*n child may love tofu. What should you do? Unless someone in your family has a soy allergy, soy products are good for the entire family. Tofu can be nestled into foods and never be discovered; it can be cooked in ways that transform it; and it can also be prepared for your child to enjoy without requiring others to partake of it. The tofu-phobe in your family may not accept such nonchalant integration of tofu into your family's life, finding ways to make disparaging comments about tofu. Gauge whether these comments are hurtful to your veg*n child or whether a sense of humor is needed to diffuse such remarks.

TRIAL PERIOD. Suggest a trial period for veg*nism—to see how it goes. Brainstorm some goals and thus some specific points for evaluation. Don't generalize and say, "Well, you tried it and it didn't work." Agree to what the expectations are:

🍃 Will they help you with a shopping list or will they go shopping with you?
🍃 Will you buy their food but they will prepare it?
🍃 Will you prepare it with them?
🍃 Will they be more involved in cleaning up?
🍃 Will they identify foods that can substitute for the protein, calcium, and iron your other family members are getting from animal protein?

If your child is not eating any animal products, it might be good to start with some basic goals that address the most important vitamins.

Take a vitamin B-12 supplement every day.
Eat at least eight servings a day of a calcium-rich food.
Eat one ounce of nuts or two tablespoons of nut butter every day.
Use ground flaxseed in one meal a day.

Here is a basis for evaluating a trial period: you and your young person agree that it is appropriate to expect that she is eating well; that she will help to insure that she is eating well as a veg*n; and finally that eating well involves her in the process of cooking. The important point is not to establish goals that can't be met, but instead to insure fairness to her needs and yours in goal setting.

VEGANIZE. It may be a new word, but "veganize" is a helpful concept for families making the change to a vegan diet or attempting to accommodate one vegan member. It refers to taking a recipe that contains meat or other animal products and making it vegan. Some recipes are easy. It's no big deal to make spaghetti with marinara sauce rather than meat sauce. And removing the beef from chili and replacing it with a soy-based ground beef substitute or just with kidney beans is an easy way to veganize. Some recipes are a little more challenging. How about mushroom Stroganoff that uses pureed silken tofu with lemon juice to replace sour cream? Or chocolate chip cookies that use ground flaxseeds to replace an egg in the recipe? You'll find that as vegan cooking becomes more comfortable and your young person explores new foods and dishes, you'll learn to veganize through trial and error. You may discover that it is fun to come up with new and creative vegan variations on old family favorites.

VEGAN PRODUCTS. Vegan products include: animal-free clothing (non-leather, non-wool, non-silk, etc.), shoes, boots, belts, bags, school supplies, and cleaning products. Many online and catalog companies sell a variety of vegan products. Looking online or at their catalog may be reassuring to you in many ways: First, you will discover that it is not as difficult as you might have imagined to obtain vegan products. Second, the fact that catalogs exist for this community of consumers suggests that it is more widespread, if not mainstream, than it might have seemed when your child first introduced the idea into your household. Finally, you have found sources for everyday needs like soaps and shampoos as well as for holiday and birthday gifts. Check out:

- PANGEA www.veganstore.com 1-800-340-1200
- VEGAN ESSENTIALS www.VeganEssentials.com 1-414-607-1953
- VEGAN STREET www.VeganStreet.com 1-866-55-VEGAN

- THE VEGETARIAN SITE www.TheVegetarianSite.com 1-520-529-8691
- VEGAN MERCANTILE www.veganmercantile.com
- www.tofurky.com or 1-800-508-8100 (for vegi deli slices and "tofurkys")
- For veg*n cookbooks and veg*n products, the Mail Order Catalog for Healthy Eating of the Book Publishing Company provides a wealth of resources. Call 1-800-695-2241 or check out their Web site at www.healthy-eating.com
- Dixie Diner, whose motto is "Health Food that Tastes like Junk Food™" offers a variety of mixes for foods such as onion soup, bean casserole, pasta primavera, "chicken" and dumplings, etc. They can be reached at Dixie USA, Inc., PO Box 1969, 15555 FM 2920, Tomball, TX 77377, 1-800-233-3688 or www.dixiediner.com

VEGAN/VEGETARIAN RESOURCES. The following groups provide information and assistance to vegans and vegetarians.

Compassion over Killing: www.cok.org
Physicians Committee for Responsible Medicine: www.pcrm.org
Vegan Action: www.vegan.org
Vegan Outreach: www.veganoutreach.org
Vegetarian Resource Group: www.vrg.org
Viva! USA: www.vivausa.org

WEB SITES. See "Vegan/Vegetarian Resources" and "Vegan Products."

WEDDINGS. See "Celebrations."

WHAT'S LEFT TO EAT? Meat and milk form two whole food groups. So what on Earth will your child eat now? Although dropping these foods from the diet may seem like a drastic change, it's not all that big a deal. For one thing, even people who include animal foods in their diet are supposed to use these foods condiment-style—just small amounts to flavor meals. They are no longer supposed to be "center of the plate" items. And as you explore vegan-style eating with your child, you'll probably be surprised at all of the choices. For starters: pasta, rice, oatmeal, ready-to-eat cereal, bread, crackers, rice cakes, fruits and vegetables (your local store probably boasts at least twenty different kinds of each), baked beans, about ten other kinds of commonly available beans, tofu, tempeh, soymilk, rice milk, almond milk, textured vegetable protein, soy "sour cream," soy "cheese," soy "cream cheese," soy "yogurt," veggie burgers, veggie hot dogs, veggie sausage, veggie "ground meat," veggie chick'n nuggets, spaghetti sauce, canned minestrone soup, peanut butter, almond butter, and wonderfully prepared foods such as hummus and tofu spread.

This is just a start and most of these foods are available at large supermarkets. If you wander into a natural-foods store or food co-op, you will hardly be able to fathom the choices. The interesting thing about vegan diets is that, because most of the world's great cultures base their cuisine on beans, grains, and vegetables, many vegans begin to explore those cuisines. So all of a sudden, it isn't just wheat in your diet, it's the wonderful Middle Eastern grain salad tabouli. And it isn't just rice and veggies, but rice and veggies and tofu, with a spicy Thai or Indonesian peanut sauce on top. It isn't just grilled Portobello mushrooms, but Portobello mushroom cap burgers with beefsteak tomatoes, lettuce, and onions; it's baked potatoes with stedda sour cream (see p. 140).

(Meat-eating parents and others might notice that some veg*ns get a bit of a confused look when you ask them what they eat. It's because veg*n diets are often so varied and interesting that many of us barely know where to begin!)

3

Nutritional Issues
for Vegetarians

by Virginia Messina, M.P.H., R.D.

When children adopt a new way of eating—and a style of eating that may look restrictive at first glance—it's natural to think about all of the potential pitfalls. But you will be pleased to know that your young vegetarian may also immediately reap some health rewards. Some research shows that vegetarian children and teens have higher intakes of fiber and of some important nutrients like vitamin C. It's likely that vegetarian children are going to be more attentive to their diet than the average meat-eating teenager—although they are still going to need guidance from you.

Meat and dairy foods are not essential in the diet. Your child will grow just as well on protein from beans and tofu as from steak and cheese. And studies of vegetarian children who eat well-balanced diets show that this is true. There are a few issues, though, that need some attention. Vegetarian diets present a little bit more of a challenge simply because they are unfamiliar to people. Once you understand a little more about this eating pattern and know what foods provide what nutrients, you will feel confident about this new style of eating for your child.

Vegetarians who don't eat any animal products require sources of vitamin B-12, calcium, vitamin D, and zinc. New findings about fats also affect vegetarians. And needs for some nutrients, such as protein and iron, are somewhat higher for vegetarians than for meat eaters. This chapter covers these issues plus others of more general interest and presents some basic guidelines for making sure your vegetarian child meets nutrient needs. It's really all you need to know to make sure your child eats healthfully. In fact, if you don't want to wade through all of it right now, you can learn the essential basics just by reading the entries on "Bone Health," "Calcium," "Calcium-rich Foods," "Calorie-dense Foods," "Dairy Products," "Eating Disorders," "Fats," "Food Pyramid," "Iodine," "Iron-rich Foods," "Minerals," "Omega-3 Fatty Acids," "Protein Needs," "Protein-rich Foods," "Vitamins," "Vitamin B-12," "Vitamin D," and "Zinc."

AMINO ACIDS. All of the proteins in food and in the body are made up of building blocks called amino acids. The body can make many of the amino acids, but nine of them are considered *essential*, which means they must be supplied by the diet. In fact, protein needs are really all about requirements for the essential amino acids (and also for nitrogen, a part of food proteins that is needed to make new proteins—like enzymes, muscle tissues, red blood cells—in the body). Plant proteins are sometimes called *incomplete* because they are short in one or more of the essential amino acids. But eating certain combinations of plant foods causes the amino acids to match up to make *complete* proteins. However, old rules about combining amino acids at meals by eating certain combinations of foods have been largely discredited. Protein experts have found that simply eating a variety of protein-rich foods throughout the day and meeting calorie needs is all it takes to get enough of the essential amino acids. Rules for getting enough protein in vegetarian diets are pretty simple. Eat a variety of protein-rich foods and make sure you get enough calories to maintain a normal weight—or for a child or teenager, to support growth.

ANTIOXIDANTS. Normal body processes involving oxygen cause the production of compounds called *free radicals*. These free radicals are thought to be involved in disease processes such as heart disease, cancer, arthritis, and even Alzheimer's disease. You can't avoid production of free radicals, but they are neutralized by dietary compounds called antioxidants. A high intake of antioxidants might lower risk for disease, protect brain function in aging, and generally promote good health. Although some animal foods contain small amounts of antioxidants, whole plant foods, particularly fruits and vegetables, are rich in them. Not surprisingly, vegetarians eat more antioxidants than meat eaters and their antioxidant intake is probably one important reason that vegetarians have lower disease risk. Some research even shows less dementia in older vegetarians. Some nutrients—vitamin C, vitamin E, and selenium, for example—are antioxidants. But there are many different kinds of compounds in plants that act as antioxidants.

ATHLETES. Teens who participate in sports may have higher calorie and protein needs, depending on the extent of their involvement. Protein needs are about one-and-one-half times higher for endurance athletes such as runners. And those who strength train may need twice as much protein as non-athlete teens. Generally, because athletes need more calories, their protein intake goes up automatically. On a well-balanced diet, they meet these needs with ease. But because strength training requires fewer calories and more protein than endurance exercise, getting enough protein can be a challenge. Vegetarian diets can meet those protein needs, but for vegans particularly it may require extra effort. Vegan athletes may need to emphasize higher protein foods in their diet, including plenty of legumes and soy products. There is no need for special amino acid supplements, but soy-based protein drinks can help some children to boost their calorie and protein intake. Make sure your young athlete is eating a well-balanced diet, though, and not just depending on supplemental drinks. Although both carbohydrates and protein are important for athletes, there is no advantage to restricting fat intake. In fact, avoiding fat restrictions can help female athletes in particular to meet calorie needs and may be important in maintaining normal menstrual function. Young athletes can include healthful higher fat foods in their diet such as nuts, nut butters, and even vegetable oils.

BONE HEALTH. Building strong bones throughout the first thirty years or so of life is important for avoiding bone disease like osteoporosis later in life. Of course, this may not be terribly compelling to the average young person. Your child can ignore all the things needed for healthy bones and feel perfectly fine for the next few decades. So it may be up to you to encourage a lifestyle that builds a strong skeleton. Bone health is fairly complex and depends on a variety of factors, not just getting enough calcium. For example, too much protein, particularly from animal sources, causes loss of calcium from the bones and therefore may increase the need for calcium. But protein is needed for healthy bones, so getting too little can also be a problem, especially for vegan girls and women. Other factors that might promote bone health include vitamin

K and possibly soyfoods. Factors that might be harmful to bones are too much sodium, caffeine, alcohol, and soft drinks. Keys to a lifetime of healthy bones are:

- A well-balanced diet
- Adequate calcium
- Adequate vitamin D either from food or sunshine
- Enough but not too much protein
- Plenty of green leafy vegetables (They provide calcium and also vitamin K, which is needed for healthy bones.)
- Soyfoods. They aren't essential for good bone health, but there is evidence that compounds in soy called isoflavones could protect bones.
- Moderate salt intake
- Exercise
- Avoiding soft drinks, alcohol, and caffeine.

CALCIUM. About 99 percent of the calcium in the body is found in the bones. But the tiny bit in the bloodstream is crucial for life and if levels drop, calcium is removed from the bones to replenish it. Teenage girls in general tend to get too little calcium for good bone health, and vegan girls and women often have diets too low in calcium. Children and teens need 1,300 mg of calcium per day. There is a lot of debate about whether vegetarians might have lower calcium needs than meat eaters. Diets high in protein from meat increase the loss of calcium from the bones so that more dietary calcium is required. But because so many factors affect calcium needs and bone health, it's too simplistic to say that vegetarians can get away with less simply because they eat less animal protein. Until we know more, nutritionists recommend that all vegetarians meet the calcium recommendations for their age group. Calcium from supplements is just as good as calcium from food.

CALCIUM-RICH FOODS. There is a difference between calcium-rich foods and foods that are *good sources* of calcium. Some calcium-rich foods also contain compounds called oxalates that bind calcium so it can't be absorbed into the bloodstream. The most common of these are spinach, rhubarb, beet greens, and chard. Good sources of calcium are broccoli, collards, turnip and mustard greens, kale, figs, fortified orange and apple juice, fortified soy- and rice milk, fortified cereals, tofu made with a calcium salt, tempeh, and almond butter. Some beans contain small amounts of calcium but, again, it isn't well absorbed. Their calcium contribution shouldn't be overlooked, but this contribution is fairly small. If your child does not use dairy products, getting enough calcium is going to initially seem like a challenge. Many vegans supplement their diet with a calcium supplement and it's fine to do this. But help your child explore new sources of calcium and incorporate more of these foods into the diet. Most vegetarian foods that are rich in calcium have a number of other important benefits. Leafy greens like collards and kale may seem pretty foreign to people in most parts of this country, but finding ways to enjoy them is worth it. They contain compounds that protect against cancer, heart disease, osteoporosis, dementia, and which help protect eyesight.

CALORIE-DENSE FOODS. Because some stages of childhood, especially the teen years, are times of rapid growth, it's important to include plenty of high-calorie, or calorie-dense foods in the diet. Good choices include nuts, seeds, and nut and seed butters, avocado, whole grains such as whole wheat bagels, baked beans and other legumes, soy products like tempeh, and dried fruits. Don't shy away from including higher fat foods like nuts and avocado in family meals. They contain healthful fats and are a good way to boost calories.

CALORIES FOR TEENS. Calorie needs vary quite a bit in children, depending on the stage of growth. For example, teens need about 50 percent more calories on a body-weight basis than adults do. But because growth occurs at stages, your child's appetite may not be the same as that of a friend's child, and your child may eat differently from month to month. For this reason, calculating calorie needs for your child is difficult. As long as children are healthy and growing appropriately, you can assume that calorie needs are being met.

CARBOHYDRATES. People often equate the term "carbohydrate" with a type of food—referring to potatoes, bread, and rice as "carbs." Carbohydrate is actually a group of chemical compounds that include starch, sugars (including the sugars that occur naturally in fruits), and some types of fiber. Grains and some vegetables are high in complex carbohydrates—starch and fiber—while dairy foods and fruits are rich in sugar, also known as simple carbohydrates. Basically, the evidence is that diets high in carbohydrates are linked to better weight control and lower risk for chronic disease. But this refers to the complex carbohydrates found in whole, unrefined grains, and to the simple sugars in fruits. "Sweets" or foods containing non-fruit simple sugars often don't contribute much to the diet other than calories. Refined products like those made with white flour do have some nutritional value but are far inferior to their whole grain counterparts. Make sure your child gets plenty of the foods that provide good carbohydrates: whole grains, bread, potatoes, fruit, vegetables, and legumes.

CHOLESTEROL. Cholesterol is a fatlike, waxy substance found only in animal foods. Plant foods never contain cholesterol. Diets too high in cholesterol may raise heart disease risk, although saturated fat has a far worse effect on the heart than cholesterol does. You may have heard that people need cholesterol in their body. While it is true that cholesterol is essential for life, the human liver makes all that is needed. There is no need for cholesterol in the diet.

DAIRY PRODUCTS/MILK. Milk has always been valued in some cultures for its calcium content. In recent U.S. history, vitamin D has also been added to milk. There is such a strong bias in the United States toward drinking milk for its calcium content that many people don't realize there are other sources of calcium. For this reason, people who don't drink milk may have calcium intakes that are too low. The fact that many people don't get enough calcium without milk doesn't mean that they can't—it just means that they don't know how. Government meal planning guidelines are partly responsible for this. Their recommendations to consume two to three servings of dairy foods daily is based on culture, practicality, and politics. There is actually no human requirement for any kind of milk. As long as people get plenty of calcium from other sources in their diets, milk- and dairy-free diets are fine. In recent years, the healthfulness of milk has been questioned. Preliminary evidence suggests it could be linked to increased prostate cancer risk in men. There is some evidence that in certain children who are predisposed to diabetes, milk could raise risk for that disease. These findings remain the subject of some debate. But compared to other sources of calcium, such as leafy green vegetables and soyfoods, milk falls short. It lacks antioxidants, fiber, vitamin K (found in leafy greens and needed for strong bones), and isoflavones (found in soyfoods and linked to bone health). So plant sources of calcium are actually better for your child than milk as long as calcium needs are met.

DIABETES. Diabetes is actually two diseases, both involving problems with carbohydrate metabolism. Type-2 diabetes is more common in older people and in overweight people. Type-1 is the form of the disease seen more often in children. It is controlled by insulin injections and diet. When a child is using insulin to control diabetes, any big change to the diet should be done under supervision of a dietitian or diabetes educator. People with diabetes can follow vegetarian and vegan diets. In fact, the lower saturated fat content and higher fiber content of vegetarian eating patterns makes them a very good choice for those with diabetes.

DYSMENORRHEA. Skipped or irregular periods is a condition known as *dysmenorrhea*. Many women experience this once in a while, but chronic dysmenorrhea can be a sign of a problem. When a woman misses three or more periods in a row, this is called *amenorrhea*. It is a fairly common condition in athletes and there is some concern that vegetarian athletes experience it more often than those who eat meat. Whether or not this is true isn't quite clear though, since not all studies show it. In teen girls in particular, amenorrhea can interfere with bone growth and raise risk for osteoporosis later in life. No one knows quite why some teens skip periods, but making sure that teens get enough calories may help to prevent this.

EATING DISORDERS. In the past, vegetarian diets have been linked with eating disorders because some girls with eating disorders adopt a vegetarian diet as a way to mask their condition. It's one of many things they do to place as many restrictions on food intake as possible. It doesn't mean that girls who are vegetarian are any more likely to develop eating disorders. If you are concerned that your child may have an eating disorder, these are the things to look for:

    🍃 Your child has continued to lose weight after being vegetarian for two or three months. At first, the weight loss can be attributed to a number of factors (such as the move from a high-fat diet) and the time it takes to learn how to create healthy vegetarian meals. But after two or three months, weight loss signals a possible problem.

&. Your child starts to skip meals regularly or says that she isn't hungry.

&. Vegetarian foods that appear to be high in calories or that have fat in them are avoided—tofu, meat substitutes, peanut butter, breads, and pastas.

&. Compulsive counting of fat-grams and calories

&. Your child weighs herself or himself frequently or reports feeling bloated when eating normal portions.

&. Ritualistic behavior around food—in the way she eats (cutting everything into minuscule pieces) or in the inflexible manner of eating, such as at a certain time.

&. Obsessive/compulsive behavior

&. Distorted body image. She comments that she needs to lose weight or is fat when she's at a healthy weight or thin.

EGGS. Although eggs are a good source of protein and other nutrients, they don't offer many of the benefits of plant foods such as fiber and phytochemicals. Eggs don't play any unique nutritional role in American diets, but they are highly valued for their functional properties in recipes. They give moisture and lightness to baked products and also help to bind other ingredients together. There are powdered egg replacers on the market, but for most recipes they really don't do the trick. A better replacement is made from flaxseed. (See "Flaxseeds.") You'll get the best performance out of egg replacers if you don't tinker too much with other ingredients in your recipe. Don't reduce the fat content of the recipe—fat adds tenderness and moisture so you'll want to take advantage of it in your egg-free recipes. And if a recipe calls for white flour, don't replace it with whole grain, which is heavier. While this doesn't sound like a very good prescription for good health, there is nothing wrong with having a nice high-fat, refined sweet once in a while.

FAST FOOD. Fast food may not be the healthiest choice, but it's fun, relatively cheap, and most children enjoy it. Vegetarians are in luck because there are a growing number of choices for them at fast food restaurants. If your child is a fan of fast foods, a vegetarian diet will be a real advantage since the vegetarian choices are far more healthful than the usual fare served at these establishments. Burger King offers a vegan veggie burger. Canadian McDonald's restaurants also have a veggie burger and there is hope that this burger will soon make its way south. Wendy's and McDonalds have veggie wraps. Salads are available at most of these outlets as well as french fries, which may or may not be cooked in vegetable oil, depending on the restaurant. While fast foods should play a small role in the diets of children and teens, an occasional outing for a veggie burger and fries is fine.

FATS. Fats have a far worse reputation than they deserve. They belong in the diet of every child, where they help provide adequate calories and improve absorption of some nutrients. Some types of fat are essential in the diet. Some people think that high-fat diets raise cholesterol levels, but only saturated fat has this effect. Moderate amounts of other fats in the diet may actually help to reduce risk for heart disease. Some vegan advocates have promoted diets that are very low in all fats because of misunderstandings about how different types of fats affect health differently. High-fat foods that play a role in healthy diets include nuts and seeds and nut and seed butters (peanut butter, almond butter, tahini, etc.), soyfoods like tempeh and tofu, and avocado. Small amounts of healthful oils like olive, canola, and flaxseed oil are fine to include in the diet. Too many fatty foods can promote obesity but moderate amounts of fat seem to help people eat more healthfully. For example, vegetables taste better when they are sautéed in a small amount of olive oil and this may help your family to enjoy important nutrient-rich vegetables more. Diets that contain moderate amounts of fat have also been shown to be more effective for weight control than very low-fat diets.

FAUX MEATS. Also called meat analogs or sometimes plain old fake meat, these products are made from soybeans and other protein-rich ingredients and are formed to mimic all types of meats—burgers, hot dogs, sausage, chicken nuggets, roast turkey, barbecued ribs—you name it. Although they are new to many people, the first meat analog was created from peanuts and flour in 1877 by vegetarian pioneer John Harvey Kellogg (he also invented peanut butter, but it was his brother who founded the famous cereal company). Called *Nuttose*, this faux meat is still sold in some specialty stores today. Some vegetarians shun faux meats—they don't want to eat anything that remotely reminds them of meat. But if your young vegetarian likes them, they can make life so easy. Nothing makes it easier to replace the meat in a favorite recipe than—well, a faux meat! Besides being convenient, they are nutritious, usually boasting a high protein content, and are often fortified with other nutrients like vitamin B-12.

FIBER. When you make the transition to a diet that contains more plant foods, it's more or less a given that fiber intake will increase. Plant foods contain fiber; animal foods don't. Vegetarian diets are as much as three times higher in fiber than those of meat eaters. This is one reason why vegetarians have a lower risk for disease. There are two kinds of fiber. The soluble type, found in legumes, fruits, and some vegetables, slows absorption of compounds such as glucose and cholesterol and helps to control blood sugar levels and reduce blood cholesterol. Insoluble fiber in whole grains and vegetables speeds the movement of foods through the digestive tract and may speed elimination of compounds that cause cancer. Both kinds are important to health.

FLAXSEED. Flaxseeds earn mention because they are unique and could be quite important in vegetarian diets. First, they have an interesting nutritional profile. They are especially rich in the omega-3 fatty acid *linolenic acid*. This essential fat can be used by the body to produce the same types of fats that are found in fish oils and that are linked to reduced risk for chronic disease. Few foods provide significant amounts of linolenic acid, so including flaxseeds, or flaxseed oil, in the diet every day can be a simple way to get enough of this special fat. But you can't snack on flaxseeds the way you might on sunflower or pumpkin seeds. They are quite tiny. They also are poorly absorbed by the body unless they are ground into a powder. Try adding ground flaxseed to hot or ready-to-eat cereals or mix them into homemade baked goods or fruit smoothies. The second reason that flaxseeds are important is that ground flaxseeds, blended with water, make a super substitute for eggs in baked goods (see "Eggs"). Grind ¼ cup of flaxseed in a blender to make a fine powder. Then add ¾ cup of water and blend until viscous. The consistency will actually be similar to beaten eggs. This replaces three eggs in any batter.

FOLIC ACID. This B-vitamin has been making news because it may help to reduce both cancer and heart disease risk. It's also necessary for healthy blood and it is crucial in early pregnancy for normal development of the embryo. Vegetarians tend to eat more folic acid than meat eaters because the foods richest in this vitamin are legumes and vegetables.

Some fruits are a great source as well. It's easier now for everyone to get enough folic acid, because foods made with enriched flour are fortified with it.

FOOD-BORNE ILLNESS. Sometimes called food poisoning, food-borne illness results from microbes that grow on food. It's quite common and the twenty-four-hour stomach flu that people sometimes experience is more often than not due to bad food. Among the worst culprits of food-borne illness are animal foods, particularly poultry. It's a given that chicken sold in the United States is likely to be contaminated with salmonella, and it's usually left up to the consumer to cook food enough to kill the bacteria. However, according to studies, much of this bacteria often ends up on countertops, drawer handles, and doorknobs and isn't that easily controlled. For most people, food-borne illness results in a few days of great discomfort. For those with compromised immune systems and for older people, it can be quite dangerous. And the illness from infection with a microbe called *E. coli,* sometimes found in undercooked beef, can also have extremely serious consequences. Some young children have died from this infection. Vegetarians have a lower risk of contracting food-borne illness, but they aren't completely safe. *E. coli* have shown up on melons and other fruits that come in contact with soil. It's a good idea to wash fruit before eating it, even if it has a protective skin that won't be consumed.

FOOD PYRAMID. Although there are a number of food guide pyramids around, the one most familiar to Americans was developed by the United States Department of Agriculture (USDA). It was designed for the average American, which means that it is useful for people who eat meat. There is a political undertone to meal-planning tools from the USDA because the meat and dairy industry both have a hand in their development. In fact, the main function of the USDA has always been to promote agricultural industries. It's not too surprising that the guide offers just one choice for meeting calcium needs—dairy foods. And nutritionists have complained that the USDA guide may help people plan adequate diets but that it doesn't help them plan optimal diets. The USDA pyramid can guide lacto-ovo vegetarians toward meeting nutrient needs, but it's not ideal for this group and it is completely useless for vegans. This book will provide you with a much better set of guidelines for vegetarians.

GRAINS. Most nutritionists agree that grains should form the foundation of the diet. Technically, grains are seeds of certain grasses. Practically, they refer to just about any food made from these seeds. When we say eat plenty of grains, we mean whole and enriched cereals, breads, and foods like pasta. Most of these should be unrefined whole grains. Refined grains are stripped of their bran layer and germ portion and this reduces their content of many nutrients and fiber. Some of those nutrients are added back, but most aren't. It's fine to include some enriched refined grains in diets, too. For example, if you prefer regular pasta to whole wheat pasta, that's okay as long as you are eating brown rice, whole wheat bread, and whole grain cereals like oatmeal.

GROWTH. Growth occurs at varying rates throughout childhood, but except for infancy, it is faster during adolescence than at any other time of life. During puberty children attain fifty percent of their adult weight and as much as twenty-five percent of their final height. Nearly half the skeleton is formed during the teen years. During the growth spurt, which takes place generally over a two-year period, nutrient needs can be twice as high as at any other time during adolescence. Fortunately, appetite follows growth. Making sure that vegetarian teens get plenty of nutrient-rich foods should help to ensure that those growth-dependent nutrient needs are met. Studies show that vegetarian children and teens grow normally.

HEALTH BENEFITS OF VEGETARIAN/VEGAN DIETS. Every major respected health organization throughout the world recommends a diet based mostly on plant foods. This means that even those who eat meat should make sure that the bulk of their calories come from healthful grains, legumes, fruits and vegetables, with animal foods playing a supporting role. It's no surprise that vegetarians enjoy better health than people who eat the average American diet. Vegetarians—including vegetarian children—have higher intakes of fiber and of some important nutrients like vitamin C. Studies of populations show that vegetarian children and adults consistently have lower blood pressure and less hypertension. Vegetarian adults also are less likely to get colon or lung cancer, to have problems with their digestive system, or to develop obesity. Vegetarians have much lower cholesterol levels and vegans have even lower levels. Vegetarian men are less likely to die from heart disease, but it's not clear that women have the same advantage. Overall, though, eating a diet that is low in saturated fat and animal protein and rich in fiber and phytochemicals is bound to make a person healthier—provided he or she is also meeting all of his or her nutrient needs.

IODINE. It's only recently that nutritionists have realized that vegans need to pay some attention to iodine in their diet. Iodine is part of thyroid hormones that regulate energy metabolism. Seafood, and sometimes dairy products, supply some iodine. People who live near the world's oceans can actually inhale some of their iodine from the mist. Vegans get most of their iodine from sea vegetables—which your child may or may not enjoy—and from iodized salt. Note that in the United States, we have a choice between salt that does and doesn't contain iodine. Make sure your child uses the type that does. Sea salt, the natural salt sold in natural foods stores, is often devoid of iodine.

IRON-RICH FOODS. If you grew up thinking meat and liver were the best ways to get iron, you might be surprised to know that vegetarians have higher iron intakes than people who eat meat. Plant foods, especially grains, nuts, legumes, dried fruits, and some vegetables, are rich in iron. One problem is that plant foods contain a compound called *phytate* that binds iron and reduces its absorption. So vegetarians absorb less iron than people who eat meat. Most likely this is not a problem, though. Vegetarians don't seem to suffer from iron deficiency any more than meat eaters do. However, teens—particularly girls—are at risk for iron deficiency whether they are vegetarian or not. So it pays to make sure your teen is getting plenty of iron. Recommendations are for vegetarians to consume nearly twice as much iron as meat eaters to make sure they are absorbing enough. But iron needs for vegetarians are probably not actually that high if your child eats a diet that maximizes absorption. Some important tips:

- Include iron-rich foods at all meals and for snacks.
- Take advantage of fortified cereals: they often offer a high dose of iron.
- Include a good source of vitamin C at every meal and with every snack. Vitamin C—and other compounds in fruits—boosts absorption of iron from plants.
- Include whole grain bread in meals. When bread is leavened, the yeast helps release the iron for absorption. So breads and

other "raised" grain products are better sources of well-absorbed iron than cereals.

🔔 Take calcium supplements between meals. When they are consumed at the same time as iron-rich foods, they can interfere with absorption.

LEGUMES. This is a tough one for some new vegetarians. For many, baked beans at a Fourth of July picnic describe the beginning and end of their experience with legumes. Legumes are dried beans, peas, and lentils. They also include the subcategory of soyfoods (tofu, soymilk, tempeh, faux meats). The fact is, to be a healthy vegetarian, your child will need to learn to enjoy some legumes. They are fairly important in vegetarian diets both from practical and nutritional standpoints. Legumes are rich in protein, fiber, iron, and B-vitamins. Some of them offer some calcium and they also provide zinc. It may take some experimentation to find dishes that are appealing. Mixing beans with grains and rolling the mixture up in a tortilla or other flat bread, topped with a sauce, is a good way to form a gradual introduction to these foods; so are more familiar dishes like bean burritos and chili.

LUNCHBOX FOODS. When you can cook, coming up with vegetarian meals is not all that difficult. But brown-bagging it is another story. Nut and seed butters—peanut, almond, cashew, soynut butters and tahini—are among the best choices for sandwiches. They are tasty, don't spoil, and are super-nutritious. Team them up with all different kinds of items for variety. Try sliced apples, cucumbers, shredded carrots, apple butter, sweet relish, bananas, and chopped dried fruit. If refrigeration is available, hummus, baked tofu, commercial or homemade tofu spreads, or mock tuna made with a faux tuna substitute or chopped beans and vegan mayo are great for sandwiches. Crackers and soy cheese or nut butter, soy yogurt, and Trail Mix all travel well. If microwaving is an option, instant soup in a cup makes a perfect fast lunch on the go. So do wraps that use up dinner leftovers. Rice mixed with beans, chopped onion, toasted sunflower seeds, and a little dressing or sauce can be heated up or eaten cold.

MEDICAL ADVICE. If you are worried that your child is missing important nutrients, your doctor can perform simple tests for deficiencies. But remember that most doctors are not nutrition experts and many may be a little mystified—or perhaps even negative—about the whole idea of a vegan diet. If you want some specific diet planning help, consider consulting a dietitian. To find one in your area or even one who can help long-distance either over the phone or by e-mail, check the American Dietetic Association's Web site at www.eatright.org. Be sure to specify in your search that you want a dietitian who has expertise in vegetarian diets. Not all dietetic experts are familiar with meal planning for vegans.

MENARCHE. Menarche refers to the beginning of menstruation. Although people often think of menstruation as the beginning of puberty for girls, it actually occurs fairly late in puberty and follows other signs of sexual development. The age of menarche in the United States has decreased during the past century and it also varies among different cultures in the world. Girls who grow up on plant-based diets get their periods much later. In addition to the obvious problems associated with earlier sexual development, earlier menarche is linked to a higher risk of breast cancer later in life.

MINERALS. Minerals play rather diverse roles in the body. For example, iron is needed to make red blood cells, which deliver oxygen to all parts of the body. Zinc is needed for more than fifty different reactions in the body including those that detoxify foreign compounds. Sodium, potassium, and phosphorus help maintain delicate fluid balances in the body. Calcium is needed for healthy bones, of course, but also for normal muscle function. Copper helps to make healthy blood. Needs for some minerals, like nickel, haven't been determined; in fact, scientists aren't even sure how some of these minerals function in the body. But there is evidence that in very tiny amounts, which are easily supplied in diets, they are important for human health. Vegan diets provide plenty of most of the minerals that children need. The four that deserve a little extra attention are calcium, iron, iodine, and zinc, so be sure to read the entries on these nutrients.

NUTRIENT NEEDS. Nutrient recommendations, like the RDAs, are set at a higher level than what most people need. This insures that almost everyone in the population will get enough. Nutrient needs also vary over the lifetime and are highest during times of growth.

Since the teen years are a time of rapid growth and development, nutrient needs are quite high for all nutrients. They are also high later in life when the body uses nutrients less efficiently. Vegetarians have higher needs for certain nutrients than meat eaters because of differences in absorption. Specifically, they need more iron, protein, and perhaps zinc.

NUTRIENTS. There are six categories of nutrients:

- Protein, which is made up of amino acids and the chemical nitrogen. Our need is for both nitrogen and for nine of the amino acids, which are called *essential* or *indispensable* amino acids.
- Fat, which has many important functions in the body. Our specific need is for two essential fatty acids, called *linoleic* and *linolenic acid*, but other kinds of fat play a role in health, too.
- Carbohydrates, which include starch, sugar, and fiber.
- Vitamins. There are thirteen of these—the B vitamins, vitamin C, and the four fat-soluble vitamins, A, D, E, and K.
- Minerals. There are at least twenty-five minerals that are required for health.
- Water. Our most crucial essential nutrient! We couldn't live a week without it.

With the exception of the mineral iron, and sometimes of vitamin D, people in developed countries do not generally have severe enough nutrient deficiencies to cause acute illness. That is not so in much of the world. Children lose their eyesight in poor countries for a lack of vitamin A in their diet. They die from lack of protein. Their growth is severely stunted due to inadequate vitamin D. But when calories are adequate, children can go for a long time on a diet that doesn't provide quite enough of all nutrients without suffering any dire consequences. However, the effects of these marginal deficiencies may be slightly compromised growth and development and a greater risk for other diseases. That's why parents strive to make sure their children eat a balanced diet. Different foods are rich in different nutrients. But it is pointless to try to memorize those sources or to try to plan diets that include good sources of each of these nutrients. Vegetarian children who eat enough calories and eat a variety of foods, including plenty of fruits and vegetables, are pretty much assured of meeting almost all of their nutrient needs. For example, you really don't need to pay a lot of attention to vitamin B-1 (also called thiamine). Children who eat bread or breakfast cereal are going to get enough. Children who regularly eat fruits will get adequate vitamin C. The nutrients that deserve some parental attention for vegetarian children are vitamin B-12, calcium, iron, zinc, vitamin D, iodine, and fats. And it is easy to meet these needs once you know how to do it. The Vegetarian Food Guide on pages 106–7 will help.

NUTRITION. Nutrition is the science of how compounds in food affect growth and health. It covers the relationship between nutrients and general maintenance of health as well as how different dietary patterns affect chronic disease. The science of nutrition is extremely complex and is based on chemistry, biology, anatomy, physiology, and physics. There are new findings from nutrition research every day. The fact that nutrition is complex and also that it is popular means that you will run across a lot of information about nutrition and much of it will be wrong. That public health messages about nutrition are sometimes influenced by the politics of the food industry serves to further cloud the issue. This means you are bound to run into some misinformation about vegetarian diets. Don't get too concerned with theories on all of the special practices required for vegetarian diets or stringent restrictions. You may read that vegetarians should restrict all fats or eat diets that combine certain foods or avoid certain food combinations. It's helpful to just stick to the basics: make sure your child gets enough calories and eats a variety of foods. Make sure he or she eats foods that provide adequate amounts of calcium, vitamin D, vitamin B-12, zinc, iron, omega-3 fats, and iodine. Include whole foods—like unrefined grains—in meals as often as possible, but don't be too concerned about occasional sweets and treats or family favorites like pasta made from refined flour.

OMEGA-3 FATTY ACIDS. The fats in fish oil that have received so much attention are long-chain omega-3 fatty acids called DHA and EPA. Eggs also have small amounts of these fats. Lacto-ovo vegetarians may get tiny amounts of these fats in their diet from eggs, but vegans don't consume any of the long-chain omega-3 fats. However, a few plant foods provide a fat called *linolenic acid*, which is also an omega-3 fat. The body can convert it to DHA and EPA. Plant foods that are rich in these omega-3 fats are ground flaxseed, flaxseed oil, walnuts and walnut oil, soybean oil, and canola oil. Any of the following are believed to provide vegetarians with adequate daily omega-3 fatty acids:

2 teaspoons of flaxseed oil
2 tablespoons of ground flaxseed
2 tablespoons of canola or soybean oil
½ cup walnuts

To maximize conversion of linolenic acid to the long-chain omega-3 fatty acids, it is important to get the right balance of other fats in the diet. Some fats can interfere with this conversion. Avoid solid fats, like margarine or shortening, and also safflower, sunflower, and corn oil. Good oils to use in food preparation are flaxseed, walnut, hempseed, and canola oils. Olive and canola oils are the best choices for cooking since they withstand heat the best.

PHYTOCHEMICALS. The prefix *phyto* refers to plants. There are hundreds of plant chemicals that have health benefits but that are not nutrients. This means they aren't essential for life but they do promote optimal health. Through a host of different activities, phytochemicals could reduce risk for cancer and heart disease, and may protect against diseases of aging such as arthritis and dementia. The discovery of phytochemicals has caused nutritionists to look at food in a new way. For example, iceburg lettuce has never been considered an especially valuable food because its nutrient content is minimal. The same goes for apples. But new studies show that these two foods contain phytochemicals that may reduce disease risk. Clearly, there is much more to plant foods than anyone ever realized.

PHYTOESTROGENS. Plant estrogens include chemicals called *isoflavones* that are found in soybeans and foods made from them and also compounds called *lignans*, which are found in flaxseeds. The so-called estrogens in plant foods are much weaker versions of the hormone produced in a woman's body. Depending on the part of the body it affects, phytoestrogens can act like estrogen or can have just the opposite effect—called an antiestrogen effect. The isoflavones in soy are a particularly hot area of study because they may reduce risk for cancer and heart disease, protect bone health, protect brain function in aging, and may even help to ease symptoms of menopause. Isoflavones also have effects in the body—particularly in regard to reducing cancer risk—that have nothing to do with estrogenic or antiestrogenic activity. So it is clear that the isoflavones have a variety of effects on the body. There is some question about whether soyfoods are appropriate for women who are being treated for estrogen-positive breast cancer.

PROTEIN NEEDS. Teens have especially high protein needs due to their rapid growth. And vegan children and teens probably have slightly higher needs for protein than their meat-eating peers because the protein in plant foods is digested less well. Depending on gender and stage of growth, children need somewhere between 50 and 75 grams of protein per day. The higher end of this range is for faster growth periods and so children with these high protein needs are generally eating more food. Making sure that children get enough food to eat, that there is variety in their diet, and that they include some legumes and/or soy products in meals, nuts or seeds, and plenty of vegetables and grains ensures that they will have adequate protein intake. The Vegetarian Food Guide gives guidelines for making food choices. Studies suggest that vegetarian children have no problems in meeting their protein needs.

PROTEIN-RICH FOODS. The concept of protein makes most people think of meat and fish. Vegetarians might conjure up an image of beans and tofu. But there is protein in most foods that vegetarians consume. In fact, except for fruits and oils, all the foods in your child's diet are likely to contribute to protein intake. Nuts and seeds are good sources of this nutrient. Grains and vegetables have less, but they still are good sources. Of course, legumes are the plant foods with the highest protein content and foods made from soybeans—tofu, soymilk, tempeh, textured vegetable protein—are the protein stars. Here are a few examples of the protein content of vegetarian foods:

½ cup tofu — 10 grams protein
½ cup beans — 7 grams
1 cup soymilk — 5–6 grams
2 tablespoons peanut butter — 7 grams
1 veggie burger — 10–15 grams
1 slice whole wheat bread — 3 grams
½ cup spinach — 2 grams

RECOMMENDED DIETARY ALLOWANCES. Nutrient recommendations are set by the government's Institute of Medicine and are now called Dietary Reference Intakes (DRI). Some nutrient recommendations are expressed as Adequate Intake (AI) when the evidence for setting recommendations is limited. When more information about nutrient needs is available, the recommendations are expressed as RDAs or Recommended Dietary Allowances.

SNACKS. Snacks play an important role in the diets of children and teens. Young people are on the go, often eating lots of pickup meals throughout the day. And because they have high nutrient and calorie needs, eating more frequently than three meals a day can help them meet those needs. Make sure you have plenty of nutritious items on hand that allow your young person to grab and go. Good choices: easy-to-eat fruit like apples, oranges, bananas, and bags of washed grapes; granola bars, whole-grain crackers and peanut butter, soy "cheese," frozen fruit juice bars, small containers of fortified soymilk, Trail Mix, homemade oatmeal or peanut butter cookies, and mixed nuts.

SUPPLEMENTS. It's best to get nutrients from food, but supplements are great insurance for everyone, especially children and teens. For certain nutrients—definitely vitamin B-12 and maybe vitamin D and calcium—supplements are crucial. There is no need to get too fancy. A store-brand multivitamin and multimineral pill is good enough.

VEGETARIAN FOOD GUIDE FOR AGES 9–18

Food Groups

Fats

2 servings
1 tsp flaxseed oil, 1 Tbsp canola
  or soybean oil, 1 Tbsp ground
  flaxseed, ¼ cup walnuts

Fruits

2 servings
1 medium fruit
½ c cut-up or cooked fruit
½ c juice
¼ c dried fruit

Vegetables

4 servings
½ c cooked vegetables
1 c raw vegetables

*Legumes, nuts, and other
protein-rich foods*

6 servings
½ c cooked beans, peas, or lentils
¼ c nuts
2 tbsp nut or seed butter
½ c tofu or tempeh
1½ oz meat analog
1 cup cow's milk
1 c soymilk
1 egg

Grains

6 servings
½ c cooked grain or cereal
1 slice bread
1 oz ready-to-eat cereal

Calcium-rich foods

When choosing foods from the
five food groups, include at least
ten servings each day of these
calcium-rich foods:

5 figs
½ c fortified fruit juice

½ c cooked (or 1 c raw) bok
  choy, broccoli, collards, kale,
  mustard greens, okra, turnip
  greens
½ c fortified tomato juice

½ c cow's milk
½ c fortified soymilk
½ cup yogurt
½ oz cheese
½ c calcium-set tofu
½ c tempeh
2 tbsp almond butter or sesame
  tahini
¼ c almonds
½ c soybeans, cooked
¼ cup soynuts

1 oz (28 g) calcium-fortified
  breakfast cereal

("c" = "cup")

USING THE VEGETARIAN FOOD GUIDE

1. Choose a variety of foods.
2. The number of servings in each group is for minimum daily intakes. Choose more foods from any of the groups to meet energy needs.
3. A calcium-rich food provides about ten percent of daily requirements. Choose ten servings of calcium-rich foods from the five food groups every day. If you don't eat ten servings of these foods, use a calcium supplement to make up the difference.
4. Be sure to get adequate vitamin D from daily sun exposure or through fortified foods or supplements. Cow's milk and some brands of soymilk and breakfast cereals are fortified with vitamin D.
5. Include at least three good sources of vitamin B-12 in your diet every day. These include 1 tablespoon of Red Star Vegetarian Support Formula nutritional yeast, 1 cup fortified soymilk, ½ cup cow's milk, ¾ cup yogurt, 1 large egg, 1 ounce of fortified breakfast cereal, and 1½ ounces of fortified meat analog. If you don't eat these foods regularly (at least three servings per day), take a daily vitamin B-12 supplement of 5 to 10 micrograms or a weekly B-12 supplement of 2,000 micrograms.
6. If you include sweets or sources of fat other than those in the Fats group, consume these foods in moderation. Get most of your daily calories from the foods in the Vegetarian Food Guide.

VITAMINS. Vitamins are little nutrients that fuel big reactions in the body. Although they have varied functions, they mostly work with the enzymes that drive all of the body's functions. Severe vitamin deficiencies have severe consequences and can even be life-threatening. Most people living in developed countries don't suffer those types of deficiencies, but even mild deficiencies can have negative consequences on health. For example, marginal intakes of the B vitamin folic acid might not cause an overt deficiency disease but it could raise risk for heart disease. Two vitamins—vitamin D and B-12—are of special interest to vegetarians.

VITAMIN B-12. Vitamin B-12 is found only in animal foods. Vegans who don't supplement their diets with this vitamin won't meet their needs. There is some evidence that lacto-ovo vegetarians should take supplements, too, even though there is some B-12 in dairy foods. There is plenty of misinformation floating around about vitamin B-12. Among the most harmful is the belief that this vitamin is found in fermented soyfoods like tempeh and miso, or in foods like spirulina. Most research shows that these foods actually contain a non-active form of the vitamin. Not only does it not meet vitamin B-12 needs, but it could also interfere with absorption of the real B-12. Vitamin B-12 deficiency causes both anemia and neurological problems. Although it is fairly rare, there is evidence that some vegans suffer deficiency symptoms associated with not getting enough B-12. Make sure your child's diet includes sources of vitamin B-12. The only options are either a vitamin pill or fortified foods. Most breakfast cereals are fortified with this nutrient. So are some meat analogs and some brands of soymilk. A type of nutritional yeast called Vegetarian Support Formula also contains vitamin B-12, but other types of nutritional yeast don't.

VITAMIN D. Sometimes called the sunshine vitamin, vitamin D isn't exactly essential in the diet. It's made in the body when skin is exposed to sunlight. But there is a growing opinion that people should include vitamin D in their diet. One reason is that too much sun exposure raises the risk for skin cancer. It's also a cause of premature skin aging. And even among those who spend time outdoors, there is the risk of not making enough vitamin D. Dark-skinned people and those who live in smoggy, cloudy, or northern areas may need much more sun exposure than others and may have difficulty making enough of this nutrient. Since vitamin D is crucial for healthy bones, it makes sense to play it safe and get some in the diet. This can be done only through fortified foods since just about the only food that provides vitamin D is fatty fish. Most Americans get it from milk, which is fortified with vitamin D by law. But there is some evidence that the vitamin D added to milk is poorly mixed so that some cartons of milk have lots of the vitamin and some have very little. Other foods that are fortified are many breakfast cereals. Vegetarians may prefer fortified soymilk since it usually contains a type of vitamin D that is not derived from animals. However, this type, called ergocalciferol or vitamin D2, may have somewhat less activity than the vitamin D added to other foods, so your child may need more than the 10 micrograms usually recommended.

WEIGHT LOSS. If your teen needs to lose weight, a vegan diet might help. Vegans tend to be somewhat slimmer than the rest of the population, although certainly vegans can still be overweight. The ideal approach to weight loss is lots of exercise and attention to sensible meal portions. Stringent dieting is bad for everyone but especially for children and teens. And fast weight loss is not a good idea during the teen years. Remember, this is a time of growth and so your child needs a diet that will provide the nutrients and energy needed for that growth. If your teen is not overweight but is losing weight on a vegan diet, this could be a sign of a problem. A month or so of weight loss due to a change in diet is not a big deal, but if weight loss continues, make an extra effort to pack some calorie-dense foods into family meals.

ZINC. Vegans have diets lower in zinc than those of either meat eaters or other vegetarians. Not only that, but zinc is absorbed less well on vegetarian diets. Nutritionists haven't paid much attention to zinc deficiency because it's not a very common problem. In some parts of the world, real zinc-related problems like stunted growth and poor sexual development are seen in deficient teens. That doesn't happen to vegans in developed countries. But there is little information about what happens when teens or others have just marginal zinc intakes—enough to avoid overt deficiency signs but perhaps not enough to support optimal function. Zinc is needed for more than fifty enzymes in the body, so it is possible that subtle things happen related to health when teens don't get enough zinc. Help your teen choose plenty of zinc-rich foods, which include whole grains (refined, enriched grains lose a lot of their zinc), seeds, and nuts. Vegetables supply some zinc as well and so do beans. Bread is better for zinc absorption than crackers and grains.

4

Underlying Facts

Philosophy, Peer Relationships, and Traumatic Knowledge

Some of the more contested issues in your household may arise when discussing the lives and deaths of domestic animals. You may feel that your child has read animal rights literature that twists the truth. On the other hand, you may be startled to hear information about chickens and laying hens and veal calves and dairy cows. You may distrust the source of the information, wondering whether it is accurate.

You or your child may want to debate very specific issues—not just the treatment of animals, but environmental issues, or the role of religion. You both may feel that the other has distorted the information available. Before falling headlong into one of these conversations, it is important to remember that the emotional content of these issues has a different resonance for your child than it does for you. This gives you quite a bit of power right at the offset—not just the power of a parent over a child, but the power of a person who has not been as deeply moved by information about the environment or animals over a person who has been deeply moved. Obviously, you have less invested in your child's vegetarianism than your child does. But why does your child care about this issue? This chapter is an attempt to help you answer that question.

I call the knowledge that a person has about the fate of animals *traumatic knowledge*. When the movie *Bambi* came out, the Disney company was accused of being anti-hunting because so many children were upset by the scene in which a hunter kills Bambi's mother. After the movie *Babe* appeared, many children and adolescents stopped eating animals. They were called "*Babe* vegetarians." Our culture protects us from the truth about the fate of animals in slaughtering. When your child watches a film or reads some material or simply thinks about what butchering entails, his reaction may be strong and immediate. The knowledge that animals are being killed to feed human beings may not seem like startling or upsetting knowledge to you. You are accustomed to it. But it may feel fresh, and startling, and painful to your child. You don't have to agree with your child to recognize that he is feeling some pain in response to this knowledge.

What does your young person need? Let's talk first about what she doesn't need. She doesn't need to be dragged to a counselor because these feelings should be taken away or "cured." She doesn't need to be mocked or teased by family members: "We're eating Bambi tonight," or "Let's have Babe for dinner." The first response, turning to counseling, overreacts to the child's feelings; the second response, teasing, is disrespectful and hurtful to your child's feelings.

Try to remember something that truly upset you when you were a child. How was that feeling received? If you remember the painful nature of criticism or trivialization, try not to pass that response on to another generation. If your feelings were accepted, you have a model for how to respond to your child.

The crucial thing about traumatic knowledge is that it demands action. In this case, the child, learning about butchering and nonhuman suffering, decides to act to stop it by becoming a veg*n. Several points about the fact that traumatic knowledge requires action are essential to understand. Trying to thwart your child's desire to respond to traumatic knowledge by becoming veg*n adds secondary crises for your child on top of this initial one—the crises of powerlessness and complicity. To be passive when one knows about suffering is upsetting; worse is to feel complicit because you are powerless to do what you want to do in response to your knowledge because authority figures restrict your actions.

Forcing your child to eat meat, even though he protests and says he doesn't want to eat a once-living animal, can be a cruel use of parental power. Your child will feel you have not tried to understand his feelings. Your child may become doubly alienated—alienated from you, his parents, because you have not heard him, and alienated from his own sense of a moral center that dictates a response to traumatic knowledge.

In this chapter, I try to offer some discussion of those things that your child may know and which may have influenced your child's decision to be a vegetarian. I chose to use two sources whose authors were not motivated by a desire to convert their readers to vegetarianism. I have tried to relay the information dispassionately, drawing upon Eric Schlosser's *Fast Food Nation* and a slaughterhouse expert. Schlosser points out in his afterword to the paperback edition of his bestselling book, "Although *Fast Food Nation* has been strongly attacked, thus far its critics have failed to cite any errors in the text." The other source I used are chapters 5 and 6 of the Humane Society of the United States report *The State of the Animals: 2001*. It can be found online at www.hsus.org/ace/13167. These chapters draw upon reports from the industries themselves as well as the United States Department of Agriculture. The material on slaughtering is written by Temple Grandin, who designs slaughterhouses.

This is background material. You and your child see the same thing differently. Using these sources, I have tried to suggest why your child sees meat eating (and perhaps the use of dairy products and eggs) in a negative way, without inserting my own opinions into the discussion.

Perhaps this chapter can help you appreciate your child's position without needing to be convinced or converted by it. Essentially, traumatic knowledge wants to be heard. As has been suggested in other entries, you can say, "You feel this way. I can see you feel strongly. I don't feel that way. But given that you can be healthy as a vegetarian, we will work with you."

ANIMALS AS INDIVIDUALS. Children often experience animals in their specificity as separate, unique individuals. They see *a* cow, not cows, they think of *that* pig, not pigs. Through an experience or through reading, adolescents have this sense of each animal's individuality reawakened. Meat is no longer separated from the fact that it comes from *a* cow, *a* pig. For them, they experience a culture that views only some animals as individuals ("pets," for instance, or the turkey that is pardoned by the President of the United States every Thanksgiving). Once animals are seen as individuals, it is discomforting to encounter the fact that most animals, especially those used for foods, are not seen this way. Once aware, it is hard not to see, especially at the dinner table. This may explain why it is over dinner that discussions get most animated. To them, an individual animal has been killed and is being consumed—an individual animal, not an anonymous being.

Simone Weil and Iris Murdoch, whose ideas are discussed under "Attention" in chapter 1, also offer you insights into the process of attention that your young person is bringing to the issue of animals, if his or her motivation for veg*nism is an ethical one. In a sense, your child has decided that animals need to be treated more like persons with needs than as *things*. She is asking the ethical question, "What are you going through?" but her question is directed not only to human neighbors but to her nonhuman neighbors.

ANIMALS AS PEERS. A new book that examines the role of animals in the development of children, *Why the Wild Things Are: Animals in the Lives of Children*, suggests that children may see animals, including domesticated animals, as "interspecies peers." Children recognize we humans are actually both human and animal. This sense of interrelatedness prompts moral questions such as "Why are we mistreating/eating our peers?" Gail Melson, the author of *Why the Wild Things Are*, explains, "Precisely because children accept animals as other living beings, they raise issues of just, fair, right, and kind conduct." Their veg*nism may evolve as their answer to their sense of connectedness. It may seem to your child an alien idea *not* to recognize our relationship with nonhuman animals. Your child may be trying to understand why you can't see the obvious. You may desire to argue him out of this position that he is holding. What you are actually doing is asking him to ignore his sense of relatedness to the nonhuman world and to disregard what it means to follow his own moral compass.

ANTIBIOTICS. Low dosages of antibiotics have been fed to domesticated animals as feed additives. Their purpose was to enhance growth. But their chronic use in animal feeds has given rise to new strains of pathogens that are resistant to antibiotics. These pathogens can infect humans as well as animals. When humans become infected with these bugs, the old antibiotic treatments are no longer effective. So overuse of antibiotics in agriculture is a growing public health problem. But now concern has been raised about the development of antibiotic-resistant pathogens, which compromise human health.

BIBLICAL PERMISSION TO EAT ANIMALS. You may believe your religion requires or encourages meat eating through its scriptures and want your child to adhere to this belief. If you are Christian or

Jewish you may turn to Genesis 1:26 and say, "Look, we were given dominion over the animals." Much debate about the meaning of the word *dominion* in Genesis 1:26 has occurred. Some scholars have shown how the word *dominion* is used elsewhere in the Bible to refer to the "dominion" the sun has in the sky. Others suggest that the word *dominion* does not include the meaning "treat cruelly." Others say that the dominion granted humans is actually within a vegan world, since Genesis 1:26 is followed three short verses later with references to the foods that God has given humans: "every plant yielding seed . . . and every tree with seed in its fruit; you shall have them for food."

It may be that Genesis 9, in which Noah is given permission to eat animals, is a compelling text. God says, "Every moving thing that lives shall be food for you." But is this permission or concession? Rabbinical scholars interpret this passage as a divine concession to human weakness. It has been pointed out that the permission does not require someone to eat animals; others have suggested that God often gives people what they want, even if it is not consistent with God's ideals. In this interpretation, the permission to eat meat would demonstrate human vanity. It has also been suggested that permission to eat meat was a temporary one; the flood had destroyed so much plant life. Good people, scholars and religious thinkers, do not have one viewpoint on this passage. But it is clear that God does not require meat eating.

God grants humans freedom; this may be a model for the role of the parent with a veg*n child—granting freedom to make decisions.

CHICKENS. This is the reason your child may decide not to eat chicken: Egg-laying chickens (called "layers") and meat-producing chickens (called "broilers") are both kept in confinement systems. Most laying hens are housed in what are called "battery cages." These cages are stacked in tiers and arranged in rows. Generally, they hold from three to ten hens. According to *The State of the Animals: 2001*: "The recommended space allowance for laying hens in some countries is 60–80 square inches per hen, barely enough for her to perform normal comfort behaviors; however, many hens are allowed less than even that meager amount."

Within the confinement space—a very large building—there may be thousands to tens of thousands of cages. Among the controversial aspects of egg production is the practice of "forced molting," when hens are deprived of food for eight to twelve days. This stimulates hens, after they have lost thirty to thirty-five percent of their body weight, to resume higher egg production. They may go through this laying cycle one additional time before being butchered. Other controversial practices include "debeaking" or beak trimming, in which the distal third or half of their beak is removed when the chicks are one to two weeks of age. Sometimes parts of the toes are removed as well. This is done with a hot blade. Since male chicks have no commercial value, they are killed. According to the United States Department of Agriculture, "219 million chicks were killed in the commercial laying industry in the United States, usually in a high-speed macerator or by gas within twenty-four hours after hatching."

Tens of thousands of broiler chickens are housed together in "either completely or partially enclosed buildings on a floor covered with bedding." Those who are "broiler breeders," that is, the parent birds, are both beak- and toe-trimmed. Their feed is restricted to prevent obesity, and water is often restricted to prevent problems with wet litters. Hens, as with laying chickens, may be force molted to enable another laying cycle. Breeding has enabled the creation of broiler chickens who are able to gain weight quickly; but they gain it too quickly relative to their leg strength, and so leg abnormalities and lameness have become more frequent problems.

CIRCUSES. Most circuses use animals as entertainment. Behind the scenes, these animals may experience a variety of unpleasant experiences from being caged to being beaten. Your child may wish to boycott circuses that use animals. Some circuses, like Cirque du Soleil, do not use animals and may be a good compromise for an entertaining family outing.

CONFINEMENT SYSTEMS. Your child's vegetarianism may have resulted from learning about confinement systems. They may want you to understand what they have learned. It can be difficult listening to them, and you may feel suspicious of their claims. What they have learned that concerns them involves the new way of raising animals for animal protein that evolved in industrialized countries after World War II. This is called "confinement" or "intensive" animal production. Until then, farm animals were raised using traditional methods that involved keeping animals in outdoor or semi-outdoor environments. These methods were very labor-intensive. Now, hardware and automation have replaced human labor for many routine tasks, and animals are kept indoors.

The Animal Welfare Issues that are raised by confinement systems, as detailed in *The State of the Animals: 2001,* include:

- Inadequate ventilation. "Harmful levels of respirable dust, heat stress (if the ventilation system cannot generate adequate air flow in hot weather), and irritating or dangerous gases (arising from manure in bedding or stored in pits below the floor) can result."
- Concrete, used as low-cost flooring material, can become slippery, causing accidents. In addition, "irregular concrete seems to predispose hoofed animals to lameness; and concrete's overall hardness may stress hooves and joints."
- Space for movement of the animals in confinement systems is minimal.

COWS. Dairy cows are housed either in intensive, semi-intensive, or a combination of indoor and outdoor environments. According to *The State of the Animals: 2001*, "Roughly 60 percent of U.S. dairy operations use tie-stall barns in which each cow is confined to an individual stall and held by a neck chain, strap, or stanchion such that she can lie down but cannot turn around." Cows are usually "spent" after four years, and then are slaughtered. But they have many complications: dairy cattle with very high milk yields appear particularly prone to mastitis, lameness, and other health problems. This causes a problem for transporting them to the slaughterhouse.

DOWNERS. "Downers" is the term for animals who are unable to walk. Transporting animals to be slaughtered who are unable to walk is a serious issue. As slaughterhouse expert Grandin reports in *The State of the Animals: 2001*, "The dairy industry has some of the worst such problems. Baby dairy calves, who are too young to walk, are not fit for transport. Downer dairy cows, those who are unable to walk, are more prevalent now than in 1994." A 1999 audit revealed that "1.5 percent of all culled dairy cows arrived at a slaughter plant down and unable to walk. In the beef industry, 0.77 percent of the cows were downers." Grandin quotes a specialist from the United Kingdom who concludes that "the typical cow's foot can no longer support its [sic] weight."

ENVIRONMENTAL ISSUES. The growth toward adulthood includes the ability to think about one's future, not just one's present situation. As a result, your young person, as part of her development, is beginning to think—and worry—about her future. Many young veg*ns see meat eating as a threat to their future because of the environmental issues that accompany animal agriculture.

Animal industries in developed countries are structured to convert vegetable proteins and other food and nonfood sources into animalized protein by passing plants, garbage, animal body parts, antibiotics, and hormones through the bodies of animals. Environmental scientists view what we call the food chain as, in fact, a food pyramid. At the pyramid's base are the plants, who are *autotrophs*—able to feed themselves from sunlight (the ultimate source of energy). Because they rely on the sun's energy for their sustenance, plants are called "primary producers." Unlike plants, human beings and the animals they consume are *heterotrophs*, dependent on other organisms for energy. Above the plants on a trophic pyramid are the primary consumers who rely on the plants for food—the herbivores and vegetarians. Above them are the secondary consumers who rely all or in part on herbivorous animals for food. At the next level are the tertiary consumers, "top carnivores" such as eagles, hawks, tigers, and white sharks.

What environmental scientists have discovered is that every time you go up a trophic level, the amount of usable energy decreases. The closer you are to the bottom of the pyramid, the more energy is conserved. One science textbook estimates that with each transfer from one trophic level to another, 80 percent to 95 percent of energy is lost. G. Tyler Miller, Jr., in *Living in the Environment: Principles, Connections, and Solutions,* explains, "Assuming a 90 percent loss at each transfer, if green plants in an area manage to capture 10,000 units of energy from the sun, then only about 1,000 units of energy will be available to support herbivores, and only about 100 units to support carnivores." He continues: "Energy flow pyramids explain why the Earth can support more people if they eat at lower trophic levels by consuming grains, vegetables, and fruits directly (for example grain → human), rather than passing such crops through another trophic level and eating grain-eaters (grain → steer → human)." For instance, 30,000 kilocalories of energy are required to produce 1 kilogram of pork. One kilogram of eggs requires 10,000 kilocalories of energy.

The trophic pyramid illustrates the basic reasons that your child has decided that environmental benefits of a vegan diet exist: essentially, a vegan diet does not pass grain through a second trophic level. As a diet becomes dependent on animal protein, it not only moves up the trophic pyramid, it requires more water and fuel as well. Twenty thousand calories of fossil fuel are required for 500 calories from 1 pound of flesh from a cow. In the United States more than one-third of all raw materials and fossil fuels consumed are used in animal production. A pound of wheat can be grown with 60 pounds of water, whereas a pound of flesh requires 2,500 to 6,000 pounds of water.

Presently, one-half of the Earth's landmass is grazed by the twenty billion domesticated animals who are being raised for meat. (See also "Manure.")

FACTORY FARMS. See "Confinement Systems."

FAMOUS VEGETARIANS. Your child may not learn this at school, and you probably didn't learn it either, but each and every day vegetarians influence our lives, from Clara Barton, the founder of the Red Cross, to former Buffalo Bills head coach Marv Levy, former-Beatle Sir Paul McCartney, television's "Mr. Rogers," playwright Bernard Shaw, Russian novelist Leo Tolstoy, artist and inventor Leonardo da Vinci, writer Henry David Thoreau, Gandhi, and the ancient Greek mathematician Pythagoras.

Like historians of earlier decades who ignored the vegetarianism of famous people, parents may think that vegetarianism is a fad. Famous vegetarians reveal that vegetarianism is not a fad but a practice that well-respected, creative, and thoughtful people have followed throughout history.

FOOD-BORNE ILLNESSES. Every day, food-borne illnesses sicken 200,000 people, hospitalize 900, and kill 14. Food-borne illnesses like mad cow disease, *E. coli* 0157:H7, salmonella, and camphlobactyr have increased in relationship to the change in food production, the centralization of meat production, and the growth of the rendering business (which transforms the fifty percent of the animal that is not edible by humans into animal feed and non-food products such as film and tires). Centralization allows for efficient spreading of fecal-contamination. Rendering resulted in the feeding of animal parts to herbivorous animals (see "Mad Cow Disease" for a discussion of this). Unlike mad cow disease, *E. coli*, salmonella, *Listeria monocytogenes*, *Staphylococcus aureus*, and *Clostridium* have all been found in hamburger meat in the United States, and all are caused by the same thing, as Eric Schlosser so delicately puts it in his book *Fast Food Nation*: "There is shit in the meat." Cattle remain in packed feedlots, which have become efficient mechanisms for "recirculating the manure." At the slaughterhouse, "a single animal infected with *E. coli* 0157:H7 can contaminate 32,000 pounds" of ground beef. Put another way, "a single fast food hamburger now contains meat from dozens or even hundreds of different cattle." It appears not only that hamburgers are especially susceptible to *E. coli* contamination but also the meat used in the school lunch programs throughout public schools in the United States. Your child may view the information on food-borne illnesses as a compelling reason not to eat meat; your veg*n may argue to you that what is unhealthy for animals proves unhealthy for humans, too.

GOD. If you believe God created nonhuman animals for humans to eat, you may force your child to eat meat. Religious beliefs are deeply held and I don't want to challenge yours. But it is important to know that just as the issue of meat eating is contested in your household, it is also contested among religious scholars, too.

You do not want your dinnertable to be a forum for evening exercises in dismantling or attacking your core religious texts. Your beliefs are important to you. But it is possible for your child to be religious and a veg*n.

To require a child to eat meat because your religion approves of it may lead her or him to reject not only meat eating but also your religion. A little tolerance in the home leads to the potential of your child discovering her own relationship to your cherished religious beliefs. Give her a chance. Books that address these issues include Richard Schwartz's *Judaism and Vegetarianism*, Richard Alan Young's *Is God a Vegetarian? Christianity, Vegetarianism, and Animal Rights*, and J. R. Hyland's *The Slaughter of Terrified Beasts: A Biblical Basis for the Humane Treatment of Animals*. (See also "Religion.")

JESUS ATE FISH . . . AND SO SHOULD YOU. In a Christian household, your beliefs may seem unreconcilable with your child's decision to eschew animal products. Perhaps your dinnertime conversations are filled with debates about what Jesus did and did not eat. What healthy theologians you are producing in your family! But it may be soul-wearying. If a referee were giving points it might go something like this. Parental point: Jesus ate fish; veg*n point: Even if Jesus ate fish, it does not appear that Jesus ate meat (the word *meat* in some translations actually meant all food at the time that the translation was made); moreover it could be that a later writer added the fact that Jesus ate fish because that writer was quarrelling with vegetarian Christian sects; Jesus ate Middle Eastern food but that does not mean we should solely eat Middle Eastern food. But you have no referee at your table, and you are the one with the ultimate power—you are the parent. Your child might raise the question, "The issue isn't what Jesus ate then, but what would Jesus do now?" You might allow your child to explore that question. It is, after all, what many Christians are teaching their children to do, to ask, "What would Jesus do?" But you have to be open to the idea that your child might decide that Jesus would not want to cause harm to animals.

The important thing that is often lost in debates such as these is that two conflicting viewpoints may each turn to the Bible not for the Bible's way, but to prove their own way is right. Since it cannot be proved that veg*nism is in conflict with the Christian message, why not allow your child to experience what it means to be a Christian veg*n? An organization exists to help him, the Christian Vegetarian Association, and a book that might assist his exploration is Keith Akers's *The Lost Religion of Jesus: Simple Living and Nonviolence in Early Christianity*.

MAD COW DISEASE. On March 20, 1996, British Health Secretary Stephen Dorrell announced the possible link between bovine spongiform encephalopathy (BSE, commonly called "mad cow disease") and Creutzfeldt-Jakob Disease [rCJD], the fatal human equivalent. An encephalopathy is any degenerative illness of the brain. It attacks the brain and gives it a spongelike consistency as the nerve cells are destroyed. Mad cow disease occurred because cows, who are ruminants, were being fed rendered parts of the bodies of sheep and cows. When cows ate the rendered remains of sheep, who commonly were infected with "scrapie," they began to come down with their own form of this "encephalopathy." A disease had "jumped species," that is, moved from one species of animal, sheep, to cows. The rendered remains of cows, fed back to other cows—including the parts that carried the infection, like the spinal cord or brains—continued to spread the disease.

With Dorrell's announcement, the fear that this disease could jump species again, from the bovine animal to the human animal, was confirmed. The human form of this disease, which one gets from eating infected meat, such as hamburgers, takes a long time to manifest itself, perhaps as many as ten years. It is degenerative and fatal. So far, the United States Department of Agriculture says that no cases of mad cow disease have been discovered in the United States. But a case has been confirmed in Canada and the practice of feeding cows rendered parts of other cows and sheep was a practice in the United States, too. Other forms of the "transmissible encephalopathy" among nondomesticated animals have been found in the North American continent, for instance, in elk. Some animal advocates argue that many "downer" cows actually have the disease.

MANURE. One cow produces as much waste as sixteen humans. Eighty thousand dairy cattle produce 7.9 million pounds of manure a day. For each pound of animal flesh 100 pounds of livestock manure must be disposed of. Unlike human waste, animal waste is not sent to a treatment plant. Huge manure lagoons near large confinement systems seep into groundwater, causing water pollution.

PIGS. According to the *New York Times*, in 1995 the average number of hogs per farm in Iowa was 400. In 2001, it was 1,300. Large-scale confinement includes using "gestation crates" for pregnant sows, in which the animals can take one step forward or backward but there is not enough space for them to walk or turn around (Florida recently outlawed these crates); "farrowing crates" for sows who have just delivered, large enough that she can stand or lie down but not large enough to turn around. "Market pigs" are housed in totally or partially enclosed buildings. Slaughterhouse designer Temple Grandin raises many issues about pig production in her chapter on "Livestock Handling and Slaughter Techniques" for *The State of the Animals: 2001*. She writes: "Single-trait selection of pigs for rapid growth and leanness has created pigs who are more fragile and likely to die during transport. I have observed that death losses during transport have tripled in the 1990s compared to the 1980s. . . . One of my biggest concerns is the possibility that producers are pushing animals beyond their biological limits. . . . Some pigs grow so fast that they have very weak bones. These pigs have large bulging muscles but are so fragile that livestock insurance companies will not sell transport insurance to producers to cover them."

RELIGION. Religious reasons for being vegetarian have existed for several thousand years. In Asian traditions, those reasons have often arisen from the ethical principle of nonharming. For Western religions, the motivation has arisen from a sense of respecting God's creation. If your religious beliefs are important to you, you might encourage your young person to explore the relationship between their veg*nism and your religion. These books may be helpful in that exploration: Rynn Berry's, *Food for the Gods: Vegetarianism and the World's Religions*, Christopher Key Chapple's *Nonviolence to Animals, Earth, and Self in Asian Traditions*, Philip Kapleau's *To Cherish All Life: A Buddhist Case for Becoming Vegetarian*, Steven Rosen's *Diet for Transcendence*, and Kerry Walters and Lisa Portmess's *Religious Vegetarianism from the Hesiod to the Dalai Lama*.

SLAUGHTERING. You and your veg*n child may disagree on the ethical issue of whether animals should or should not be slaughtered. For the meat eater, humane slaughter is the guarantee that cruelty is avoided in the killing of animals. To the vegetarian, there is no such thing as "humane slaughter." This entry is not going to address that disagreement but will instead address the practical issues involved in guaranteeing there is no cruelty to animals being killed. Currently, most animals are killed through a mechanized system, rather than, as in earlier times, by the local village butcher. The exception is animals killed through ritual slaughter—either Kosher or Halal—in which an unstunned animal's throat is cut. The Humane Slaughter Act and its 1978 amendments do not cover the slaughter of poultry or ritual slaughter. Because of the more consistently predictable size of chickens, much of the slaughtering process is mechanized. But whether is it humane or not is not addressed by federal agencies since poultry are not covered under the act.

Discussion of the slaughter of animals must address several interrelated aspects of killing: stunning techniques (and the maintenance of stunning equipment), line speed, the size of the meatpacking plant, the psychology of the worker, and management.

How are animals stunned before being killed? Cattle are stunned by a captive-bolt stunning pistol that fires a steel bolt into the head. The goal is for the cattle to be stunned with one shot. Sometimes, if the pistol misfires or the stunner errs, it will take two. Pigs are either stunned electrically or through the administration of carbon dioxide. Carbon dioxide stunning is not instantaneous and its effectiveness varies depending on the breed of pig.

After the animal is stunned, a worker grabs one of the animal's hind legs, shackles the leg to a chain, and the chain hoists the animal into the air. The "sticker" slits the neck of the animal, aiming for the artery that will kill the animal instantaneously. Through this process, the upended animal's heart aids in the butchering process by pumping the blood as it drains from the body.

Temple Grandin, who designs slaughterhouse equipment and has visited numerous slaughterhouses in her efforts to create a more humane environment, reports in chapter 5 of *The State of the Animals: 2001*, "In 1996 only 30 percent of the plants stunned 95 percent of their cattle correctly—with one shot." She reports, "I have observed many abuses, such as broken stun guns, the dragging of downed, crippled animals, and deliberately driving animals over the top of a downed animal; but in the vast majority of plants, I have never observed live pigs going into the scalder or live cattle being dismembered."

What is line speed? Line speed is the number of animals killed during a one-hour period. Line speed has increased in the past thirty years. According to *Fast Food Nation*, "The old meatpacking plants in Chicago slaughter about 50 cattle an hour. Twenty years ago, new plants in the High Plains slaughtered about 175 cattle an hour. Today some plants slaughter up to 400 cattle an hour—about half a dozen animals every minute." Line speed may cause the workers to be overworked, which may cause stress, bad behavior, and injury.

With the concentration of slaughterhouses into meatpacking factories, the type of worker employed has changed. Before, a union-represented laborer might work his entire life at one plant; now, plants are characterized by low wages, a high turnover rate, and the enlisting of migrant workers from other countries. According to Schlosser, "The Immigration and Naturalization Service estimates that about one-quarter of all meatpacking workers in Iowa and Nebraska are illegal immigrants." Impoverishment in other countries has made the most dangerous meatpacking jobs attractive. Again, Schlosser: "The injury rate in a slaughterhouse is about three times higher than the rate in a typical American factory. Every year more than one-quarter of the meatpacking workers in this country—roughly forty thousand men and women—suffer an injury or a work-related illness that requires medical attention beyond first aid."

Each aspect—stunning techniques, line speed, the size of the plant, management, the psychology of the worker—impinge on the other. If there is pressure to keep the line speed high, the stunners may have less time to stun properly, or as Temple Grandin remarks, stunner "operators may not always be so careful about making sure that the animals are stunned properly." Small plants may be the location of egregious abuses, as she explains: "Doing something terrible like skinning a live head is more likely to occur in a small plant where the same person performs both bleeding and the initial stages of skinning."

Plants can be well managed or poorly managed. If poorly managed, there is no one acting, in Grandin's terms, as a "'conscience' to control behavior" and employees may become rough. Grandin believes there are three basic types of workers in a slaughterhouse: those who do their jobs like box staplers on an assembly line, holy people who perform their job as a sacred ritual, and sadists. Without good management, sadists are not weeded out.

Vocalization, that is, moos and bellows, announce that the cattle or pig is experiencing stress or pain or both. Researchers have correlated vocalization with handling problems such as "excessive electric prod use, slipping and falling, missed stunner shots, and excessive pressure from a restraint device." Vocalization is an inverse measurement of a plant's humane handling of animals.

Slaughterhouses produce waste—fat, carcass waste, and fecal matter. This waste is being dumped into rivers in the United States at the rate of more than two tons an hour and is several hundred times more concentrated than raw waste.

VEAL CALVES. The United States produces one-fourth of the world's veal. Male calves are, in a sense, a byproduct of the dairy industry. Cows, to produce milk for humans, are impregnated frequently to maintain milk production. Because the cow's milk production is intended for humans, most calves are weaned within twenty-four hours of birth. Either the male calves are killed shortly after being born, or they are raised to become meat. According to *The State of the Animals: 2001*: "Calves may be raised to an age of four months or older on a grain-based diet and marketed as 'pink veal' or 'baby beef,' or they may be fed a low-iron, milk-based, or milk-like diet, and marketed as 'white' or 'special-fed' veal. These calves may be kept in small groups, but white-veal calves are more commonly kept in individual stalls that limit their movement and prevent them from turning around."

VEG*NISM. Veg*nism is a popular choice for abbreviating "vegetarianism or veganism." A vegetarian is someone who does not eat dead animals. It is a term that was coined in 1847. Whereas there has been some general erosion to the term "vegetarian," so that for some people it has come to mean someone who does not eat red meat or someone who does not eat four-legged animals, in fact, vegetarians do not create a hierarchy of which animals are acceptable to eat. "Pollo-vegetarians" or "pesco-vegetarians," that is, "chicken-eating vegetarians" and "fish-eating vegetarians" are misnomers that have entered the English language as medical studies revealed health concerns related to the consumption of red meat. You may find yourself asking your child, "Well, why can't you eat chicken?" or "Why can't you eat fish?" because you have heard that some vegetarians do eat chicken and fish. You are seeking an understanding of why your young person has taken this vegetarian concern so much further than others you might have met or heard of. Your child may hear the question as yet another example of a failure to communicate. It is often easiest to define vegetarianism in the negative: vegetarians do not eat anyone who bleeds, or vegetarians do not eat anyone who had a mother, or vegetarians do not eat anything with eyes (except potatoes). Using these "definitions," it becomes clear why chicken and fish are excluded by vegetarians.

Recently, a retired professor, Stanley Sapon, provided a definition of veganism for Joanne Stepaniak's *The Vegan Sourcebook* that might be helpful for you:

> *Veganism is an ethic that is committed to reverence and respect for all life and the planet that sustains it. Veganism brings with it the joy of living with peace of spirit, and the comfort of knowing that one's thoughts, feelings, words, and actions have a strongly benevolent effect on the world.*

Of course, within your household, veganism may not strike you as being motivated by compassion because of the friction that it is causing. You might ask your young person to select a time when she would sit down and explore with you her thoughts about this definition.

ZOOS. Your child may refuse to go to one. Facing captive animals, no matter how scenic the cages, may feel unbearable. If your child's class is going to the zoo, and this is not something your child feels comfortable with, devise an alternative experience of "looking at" animals. Perhaps your child can go into the backyard, to a park, or near a pond or a lake to observe all the nonhuman lives there: birds, squirrels, worms, and bugs. Your child could keep a log of the nonhuman life she observes and share this with her teacher and her class the next school day.

5

What's Left to Eat?

Recipes for Surviving and Thriving

Here are some recipes that Virginia Messina and I selected to provide a jumping-off point for cooking with and for a veg*n. We turned to recipes we have found reliable in our own lives, and added to them a few recipes from some of our favorite veg*n cooks. Don't be fooled by categories! You can use many of the recipes in the breakfast section both for brunches and for relaxed suppers. Some salads can function as main dish meals.

Since breakfasts seem heavily associated with milk and eggs, we have tried to provide recipes that can replace the old tried-and-true, reliable breakfast standbys (like pancakes and French toast) while also suggesting other interesting possibilities (like Miso Soup or Couscous with Cinnamon and Raisins). On days when children are often rushed at breakfast time, try a smoothie. As for main dishes, there are plenty to experiment with—some using very familiar foods, so that no one has to be shocked by the change. We have used pasta, of course, but also grains such as couscous, millet, and quinoa. Some recipes invite you to experiment with tastes and textures that you might not be familiar with. You and your child can decide together how to balance the competing needs in your family. It can be a family affair to prepare food as well as to eat it. Unless otherwise noted, the following recipes have been adapted by Ginny and Carol. The cookbook authors and vegan chefs who have shared with us their wonderful recipes are:

Shirley Wilkes-Johnson—an amazing vegan chef in Texas and a vegan cooking instructor.

Beverly Lynn Bennett—known as "The Vegan Chef"—has created a cookbook called *Eat Your Veggies! Recipes from the Kitchen of The Vegan Chef* that may be downloadable as a PDF file at www.veganchef.com.

Joanne Stepaniak—the author of *Vegan Vittles*, *The Vegan Sourcebook*, *Being Vegan*, and many indispensable vegan cookbooks.

Jennifer Raymond—the author of *The Peaceful Palate*, a consistently popular vegan cookbook. Her recipes are easy to prepare and always wonderful, delicious, and enjoyable.

Kay Bushnell—a vegan chef, teacher of vegetarian cooking, and the author of *Burgers, Turnovers, and Other Treats*.

Animal Place—a sanctuary for abused and unwanted "farm" animals. Pigs, goats, cows, sheep, rabbits, hens, roosters, and other animals roam freely on 60 acres. Animal Place hosts open house events, vegetarian cooking classes, and an annual Veggie Cook-Off. The winners are published in their yearly *Veggie Cook-Off Cookbook*. Animal Place, 3448 Laguna Creek Trail, Vacaville, CA 95688, www.AnimalPlace.org.

DFW Vegetarian—the vegetarian umbrella group for vegetarians in the Dallas Fort Worth area: dfwnetmall.com/veg/. Terry Jensen has been funneling recipes to interested vegans for several years now.

Lagusta Yearwood—a talented young vegan chef, who has just finished studying at the Natural Gourmet Cookery School in New York City. If you are lucky enough to be living in the New York City area, she provides catering and meal delivery. Contact her through www.lagusta.com.

BREAKFAST

Basic Muffins

Yields 12 muffins

½ cup soft tofu
6 teaspoons Ener-G egg replacer
½ cup canola oil
¾ cup maple syrup or 1¼ cup
 Fruitsource
1 ripe banana
1½ cups whole wheat pastry flour
½ cup soy flour
¼ cup oat bran (make your own
 with oats pulverized in a blender)
Dash of salt
2½ teaspoons baking powder
½ teaspoon grated nutmeg
1 teaspoon ground cinnamon

Mango Muffins

2 mangoes, cut into ½-inch cubes

Carob Muffins

⅛–¼ cup soymilk for thinning
½–¾ cup carob chips
1 tablespoon vanilla

Lemon Poppyseed Muffins

3 tablespoons poppy seeds
Zest of 3 small lemons, minced
⅓–½ cup lemon juice

1. Preheat oven to 400° F. Oil 12 muffin cups. Put tofu, egg replacer, oil, sweetener, and banana into a food processor. If you are making lemon poppy seed muffins, add the lemon juice; if you are making carob chip muffins, add the soymilk and vanilla. Cream together.
2. Combine the flours, oat bran, salt, baking powder, nutmeg, and cinnamon in a large bowl. Make a well in the center of the dry ingredients and add the banana mixture. Using a spatula, quickly fold in the banana mixture. Don't overmix.
3. Depending on which muffins you are making, add either the mango, carob chips, or lemon rinds and poppy seeds. Fold them into the batter.
4. Spoon batter into muffin cups. Fill each cup about two-thirds full. Bake for 25 to 30 minutes. The muffins should be lightly browned. A toothpick inserted into the center of the muffin should come out clean. Cool briefly in pan, then remove.

Cranberry Muffins

Serves 6

2 cups whole wheat pastry flour
1 tablespoon baking powder
½ cup Sucanat
1 egg replacer
2 tablespoons olive, walnut, or
canola oil

1 cup orange juice with
  2 tablespoons maple syrup
½ tablespoon vanilla
1 tablespoon orange peel
1 cup cranberries

1. Preheat oven to 350°. Sift together the flour, baking powder, and Sucanat. If the Sucanat is lumpy, rub it through the sifter.
2. In a large bowl, beat together the egg replacer and the oil. Gradually add the orange juice and maple syrup and mix well. Add the vanilla and orange peel and mix well. Add the flour mixture and beat with a wooden spoon just enough to mix well. Fold in the cranberries.
3. Turn the batter into muffin cups. Bake for approximately 13 minutes until a toothpick inserted into the center of the bread comes out clean.

for Cranberry Bread:

Turn the batter into a well-oiled and floured loaf pan, 4½ × 8½ × 2½ inches. Bake at 350° F for 40 minutes or until a toothpick inserted into the center of the bread comes out clean. Let the bread cool in the pan for about five minutes, then remove it from the pan to cool on a rack.

Miso Soup

Serves 4 to 6

This is a light, delicious, warming soup.

2-inch strip kombu
6 cups water
12 ounces silken tofu

3 tablespoons white miso
½ cup sliced scallion

1. Place kombu in water and bring to a boil over medium heat.
2. Add tofu and simmer for five minutes. Reduce heat.
3. Place miso in a cup, stir a little broth into the cup, and mix until it is smooth. Stir into the soup and cook at low heat for another minute or two.
4. Add scallions and serve.

Variations: If you don't have the kombu, don't let that stop you. Add 1 teaspoon soy sauce instead. You can also use 1½ tablespoons white miso and 1½ tablespoons red miso for a delicious taste. For a more substantial winter soup add 1 cup diced winter squash with the kombu, or corn with the tofu.

Scrambled Tofu

Serves 4

This cooks up great in an electric skillet!

1 tablespoon olive oil
3 garlic cloves, minced
8–10 medium mushrooms, sliced
½ cup carrots, grated
½ cup scallions

¼ teaspoon turmeric
3 tablespoons nutritional yeast flakes
1 pound regular firm tofu, crumbled
1 tablespoon soy sauce
1 cup spinach leaves

1. Heat the oil over medium-high heat, then sauté the garlic and mushrooms until they are golden on one side. When you flip the garlic and mushrooms over, add the carrots and scallions. Sauté them together for about two minutes.
2. Add the tofu, nutritional yeast flakes, turmeric, and soy sauce. Stir them together and continue cooking for about five minutes.
3. Add spinach, and let it cook for about one minute. It will become slightly wilted but still hold its shape.
4. Serve and enjoy.

Banana Blueberry Pancakes

Serves 4

1½ cups white flour
1 teaspoon salt
3 tablespoons sugar
2 teaspoons baking powder
1½ tablespoons flaxseed

1 tablespoon canola oil
1½ cups soymilk
1 medium banana, thinly sliced
1 cup fresh or frozen blueberries
¼ cup water

1. Combine the flour, salt, sugar, and baking powder in a medium-sized bowl.
2. Place the flaxseeds in a blender and blend at high speed until they are ground into a fine powder. Add the water and blend on medium until thick, about one minute.
3. In a separate bowl, combine the flaxseed mixture, canola oil, soymilk, sliced banana, and blueberries.
4. Pour into dry mixture and mix with a few swift strokes.
5. Cook the pancakes on a lightly oiled, nonstick pan or griddle until lightly browned on both sides. Serve with fresh fruit, maple syrup, or applesauce.

Banana French Toast

Serves 4

2 ripe bananas
1 cup fortified soymilk

8 slices bread
Canola oil

1. In a blender, blend the bananas and soymilk until completely smooth.
2. Pour into a large bowl.
3. Dip the pieces of bread into the banana mixture and fry in a lightly oiled, nonstick pan until browned on both sides.

Smoothies

Smoothies, an irresistible combination of frozen fruit with liq-uid, are quick, soothing, healthy, nourishing, and fun to make. A variety of smoothies can be created from a basic understanding of how they work and what is at the core of their existence: frozen bananas. Freeze bananas before they turn completely limp and brown. Freeze them by peeling them and keeping them in plas-tic bags. Then it's simply a matter of one, two, three.

1. Frozen bananas

plus

2. liquid: soymilk or rice milk or juices (singly or a combination): apple/orange/pineapple

plus

3. frozen or fresh fruit: strawberries, mangoes, raspberries, blueberries, or pineapple

Optional: You can add ½ cup of silken tofu for protein; ice; sweetener (including jams)

Examples:

- Frozen bananas, soymilk, a couple tablespoons of raspberry jam
- Frozen bananas, orange juice, soymilk, tofu, a little vanilla
- Frozen bananas, pineapple-coconut juice, frozen blueberries
- Frozen bananas, mangoes, soymilk, a little sweetener
- Frozen bananas, papaya juice, peaches
- Frozen bananas, strawberries, soymilk
- Frozen bananas, strawberries, apple juice

Place all ingredients into the blender and process on high speed. Stop and check to make sure that all the fruit has been blended up; dip a spatula into the mixture to help the fruit move to the center. Then blend again. The smoothie will be smooth and thick.

Couscous with Cinnamon and Raisins

Serves 2

¾ cup water
¼ cup orange juice
½ cup whole wheat couscous
¼ cup raisins

½ banana, thinly sliced
2 tablespoons apple juice concentrate
¼ teaspoon cinnamon

Put all ingredients in a saucepan, stir to mix, and bring to a boil. Lower heat, cover, and cook for five minutes. Let sit for another five minutes. Then fluff with a fork and serve.

Biscuits and Gravy

Soy "Buttermilk" Biscuits

These are absolutely the best biscuits. Great with jam, or use with the gravy recipe that follows. The biscuits are from my book Living among Meat Eaters.

A scant 1 tablespoon apple cider
   vinegar
¾ cup soymilk
1 cup white flour
1¼ cup spelt or pastry flour

¼ teaspoon baking soda
1 tablespoon baking powder
½ teaspoon salt
⅓ cup safflower oil

1. Preheat the oven to 450° F.
2. Measure the apple cider vinegar and place into a measuring cup. Pour the soymilk in until it measures ¾ cup. Leave to curdle while combining the dry ingredients.
3. Sift together the flours, baking powder, baking soda, and salt into a mixing bowl. Make a well in the center, and pour in the oil and soy "buttermilk." Use a fork to combine until mixed. But do not overmix the biscuits. Mix quickly and conservatively.
4. Lightly flour a surface and turn the dough onto it. Knead it gently a few times. Pat the dough so that it is about ½-inch thick. Using

a biscuit cutter or a glass, cut the dough into 10 to 12 biscuits. Place them so that they touch each other on an ungreased baking sheet.

5. Bake for 10 to 12 minutes, until golden brown. Serve immediately.

Gravy

3 tablespoons soy margarine
3 tablespoons olive oil
⅓ cup flour
½ cup nutritional yeast flakes
1½ cups unflavored room temperature soymilk (you can use more soymilk; reduce the broth accordingly)

1½ cups room temperature vegetarian broth
Salt
Pepper
Soy sauce

1. Melt the margarine and warm the oil.
2. Add the flour and the yeast and mix together, letting them brown a little over medium-low heat. Don't let them burn.
3. Slowly add the liquid, stirring continuously as the gravy thickens. Adjust the taste with salt, pepper, and soy sauce.

⚬≈⚬

Soy "Buttermilk" Skillet Corn Bread

Serves 6

I have adapted this recipe from Deborah Madison. You need a cast-iron skillet for this delicious recipe. Serve it warm with molasses or jam. My son Ben thinks this recipe is great.

2 cups unflavored soymilk
2 tablespoons apple cider vinegar
3 tablespoons margarine
1 cup flour
1 cup stone-ground white or yellow cornmeal
1 teaspoon baking powder
½ teaspoon baking soda

½ teaspoon salt
½ cup egg substitute (see p. 137) or equivalent of two eggs from Ener-G Egg Replacer
2 tablespoons sugar
1 cup of soy cream (White Wave makes a very good one.)

1. Preheat the oven to 375°F. Put the margarine into a 10-inch skillet and place in the oven. The margarine will melt as the oven heats up.
2. Put apple cider vinegar in a 2-cup measuring cup. Add the soymilk until it reaches the 2-cup mark. Put aside to allow the soymilk to curdle.
3. Sift the dry ingredients into a large bowl.
4. In a blender, pulse together the egg substitute, the sugar, and the soy "buttermilk."
5. Remove the skillet from the oven, spread the margarine so that it covers the sides of the skillet, and then add any remaining to the liquid ingredients.
6. Pour the liquid ingredients into the dry ingredients. Don't stir for long, only long enough to ensure that the batter is smooth.
7. Pour the batter into the hot skillet.
8. Pour the cup of soy cream over the batter. Don't stir it. It will slowly seep through the cornbread as it bakes and the result will be a moist, creamy bread with the hint of custard on top.

STEDDAS AND SAUCES

Egg Substitute for Baked Goods

Yields the equivalent of 3 eggs

¼ cup flaxseeds   ¾ cup water

1. Grind flaxseeds in blender for about two minutes, until pulverized.
2. Add water and blend for one minute until the mixture is thick. Use ¼ cup of flax mixture for each egg.

Tofu "Feta Cheese"

1 pound hard (firm) tofu, drained
   and pressed
⅓ cup olive oil
¼ cup apple cider vinegar

1 teaspoon salt
1 teaspoon dried basil
¼ teaspoon garlic powder
¼ teaspoon black pepper

Crumble or cube tofu and add remaining ingredients. Use this in almost any recipe where you would use feta cheese.

Copyright © Shirley Wilkes-Johnson

Tofu "Ricotta"

Yield: 1 pound of Tofu "Ricotta"

> *Of all the tofu "ricottas" I have tried, this is by far the most delicious and creamiest. My teens love to eat it fresh from the food processor! I have adapted it from Myra Kornfield's excellent book* The Voluptuous Vegan.

1 pound tofu, pressed for 30 minutes
6 tablespoons extra-virgin olive oil
4 tablespoons lemon juice
½ teaspoon salt

4 garlic cloves, peeled
2 teaspoons mellow barley miso
2 tablespoons fresh rosemary,
   chopped

1. Fit a food processor with a metal blade. Add to it the tofu, oil, lemon juice, salt, garlic cloves, and miso.

2. Process, pausing to scrape the sides. When the tofu is smooth, add the chopped rosemary and pulse briefly to mix it in.
3. Add the chopped rosemary and pulse to combine.
4. Remove from the processor. Use in lasagna, manicotti, or ravioli.

Tofu Ranch Dressing

Yield: approximately 2 cups Dressing

1 12-ounce box silken soft tofu
¼ cup vegetable oil (optional)
1 tablespoon lemon juice
1 tablespoon sugar
1½ teaspoon yellow prepared
  mustard

1 teaspoon apple cider vinegar
½ tablespoon salt
1 teaspoon parsley flakes
½ teaspoon black pepper
½ teaspoon garlic powder
¼ teaspoon onion powder

Combine all ingredients in a blender and blend until smooth and creamy. Use over baked potatoes and salad.

Copyright © Shirley Wilkes-Johnson

Caesar Salad Dressing

Makes 2 cups Dressing

4 large garlic cloves, halved
1 tablespoon Dijon mustard
6 ounces silken tofu
3 tablespoons red miso
2 tablespoons nutritional yeast

⅛ cup lemon juice
½ teaspoon salt
1 pinch fresh-ground black pepper
1 cup olive oil

1. In a food processor or blender, blend the garlic, mustard, tofu, miso, yeast, and lemon juice. Add the salt and pepper.
2. As the machine is running, *slowly* pour in the olive oil. The dressing will emulsify as the olive oil is added. Serve or refrigerate for up to a week.

Orange Tahini Sauce

Makes 2 cups

> *Serve over slightly spicy bean and grain dishes.*

3 tablespoons canola oil
½ cup finely chopped onion
1 clove garlic, minced
1 cup tahini
½ cup orange juice

1 tablespoon tamari soy sauce
1 teaspoon firmly packed brown
   sugar
½ teaspoon salt
Water

1. Sauté the onion and garlic in the canola oil over low heat until the onion is tender, about eight minutes.
2. Stir in tahini and reduce heat to very low. Cook, stirring constantly, for five minutes.
3. Stir in the orange juice and enough water to produce desired consistency.
4. Add remaining ingredients. Increase heat and simmer until sauce is heated through.

Nacho Sauce

Yields approximately 2 cups

½ cup nutritional yeast flakes
½ cup flour
1 teaspoon salt
2 cups water

¼ cup margarine
½ teaspoon garlic powder
1 can Ro-Tel tomatoes or 1 small jar
   mild picante sauce

1. Mix dry ingredients in a saucepan; add water and cook over medium heat, whisking, until it thickens and bubbles. Cook one minute.
2. Remove from heat and add margarine.
3. Blend tomatoes for two seconds to coarsely chop. Add to sauce. Serve warm with chips.

Tofu "Cottage Cheese"

Yields 2 cups

1 pound firm tofu
1 tablespoon olive oil
1 tablespoon apple cider vinegar
2 tablespoons lemon juice
1½ tablespoons minced onion

1 tablespoon minced chives
2 teaspoons minced dill
2 tablespoons nutritional
   yeast flakes
½ teaspoon salt

1. Blend half of the tofu and the other ingredients in a blender or food processor until creamy. Transfer to a bowl.
2. Mash the remaining tofu with a fork and then mix into the blended ingredients. Combine well. Adjust seasonings and refrigerate.

Tofu Sour Cream

1 12-ounce package Mori Nu firm
   silken tofu
4 tablespoons lemon juice
5 tablespoons canola oil

1½ teaspoons salt
1–2 scallions, white part only
1 teaspoon rice vinegar
2 teaspoons mustard

1. Blanch the tofu by dropping it into boiling water and cooking for about four to five minutes.
2. Combine the ingredients in your blender or food processor. Process until smooth and creamy.

SANDWICHES AND OTHER LUNCH POSSIBILITIES

Instant Pizzas

Pita pizza or English muffin pizza

1. Take a pita pocket or an opened English muffin.
2. Swirl some veg*n tomato sauce on top.
3. Sprinkle with nutritional yeast flakes.
4. Add veggies/spinach/artichoke hearts.
5. Warm in a toaster oven.

Basic Sandwiches

1. Select bread/roll/pita pocket/tortilla/ "hoagy" roll/bagel, or bun.

Choose the centerpiece to your sandwich:

2. Veggie deli slices/marinated baked tofu/tofu salad/hummus/mock tuna, or a spread

Add to it:

3. Lettuce/tomatoes/sprouts/scallions/avocados/guacamole

Garnish with:

4. Veg*n mayonnaise/mustard/salsa/horseradish/salad dressing/barbecue sauce

Optional: grated carrots/olives/sliced cucumber/red onions/roasted red peppers

Hummus

Makes 6 sandwiches

¼ cup fresh parsley
½ cup tahini
¼ cup freshly squeezed lemon juice
1–2 cloves garlic

1 15-ounce can chickpeas,
    drained
Salt to taste
Cayenne pepper to taste

Process the parsley in a food processor until well chopped. Add the remaining ingredients and process until smooth.

Mock Tuna

Makes 6 sandwiches

2 15-ounce cans chickpeas, drained,
    or 4 cups cooked chickpeas
½ cup Vegenaise eggless mayonnaise
2 tablespoons freshly squeezed
    lemon juice

1 tablespoon kelp powder
1 stalk celery, coarsely chopped
1 small onion, finely chopped
Salt and pepper to taste

Process the chickpeas in a food processor for a few seconds until coarsely chopped. Transfer to a bowl and add the remaining ingredients. Mix well, adjusting seasonings if desired.

Veggie Burger Wrap

Makes 1 wrap

1 veggie burger
2 tablespoons tahini
2 tablespoons toasted sunflower seeds

Fresh spinach leaves
1 10-inch whole wheat flour tortilla
    or chapati

Cook the veggie burger according to package directions. Cut or crumble into small pieces. Place in the tortilla and top with the tahini, sunflower seeds, and spinach. Roll up as for a burrito.

Black Bean Wrap

Makes 1 wrap

¼ cup black beans, cooked
2 tablespoons chopped green
   olives
1 tablespoon finely chopped onion

1 teaspoon fresh lime juice
Salsa
1 10-inch whole wheat flour tortilla
   or chapati

Heat the beans in a microwave oven or on the stove. Mash the beans slightly with a fork and mix in the olives, onions, and lime juice. Spread on the tortilla, top with salsa, and roll up for a burrito.

Tofu Sandwich Spread

Makes 4 sandwiches

1 pound firm tofu, well drained
1 tablespoon finely chopped onion
¼ cup finely chopped celery
¼ cup Vegenaise eggless mayonnaise
1 tablespoon sweet pickle relish
1 teaspoon prepared mustard

1 tablespoon dried parsley
Salt and pepper to taste
¼ teaspoon turmeric (optional)
Optional: chopped carrots, chopped
   zucchini, or 1 tablespoon
   Anaheim chilies, canned or fresh

Mash tofu coarsely with a fork. Stir in the onion and celery. In a separate bowl, combine the remaining ingredients. Add to tofu and mix thoroughly. Serve in a whole wheat pita pocket.

Hot Tofu Sandwich

Baked tofu (p. 144) makes an excellent sandwich with condiments.

Onion, thinly sliced
Bell pepper, thinly sliced

Canola or olive oil
Herbs or spices

1. Warm oil in skillet. Add thinly sliced onions and bell pepper. Add any additional spices you enjoy, such as oregano or basil.
2. When onions and bell pepper are ready, add slices of baked tofu to warm and coat with spices. Enjoy a hot sandwich.

Baked Tofu

1-pound package of firm tofu   Spices (optional)
Salt and pepper

1. Preheat oven to between 325° and 375° F.
2. Slice tofu into eight pieces.
3. Rinse and place in one layer on a nonstick cookie sheet or other flat pan.
4. Season with salt and dry spices, then rub in spices if you wish.
5. Bake until tofu puckers and slightly browns on one side.
6. Turn and brown the other side if desired.
7. Store in covered container (no water) until ready to use.

Your chewy tofu is now ready to add to almost any dish. You can also eat a slice in a sandwich. Cook enough for one week, although baked tofu usually lasts at least 10 days in your refrigerator. Spoiled tofu smells awful, so use your nose when in doubt.

Tip: I put a stainless steel knife under one side of the cookie sheet. This slight angle makes water run to the end of the pan where it evaporates. That's not totally necessary, but it hastens the baking process.

Spices: Use salt and pepper as your only seasonings unless you have a particular dish in mind when you bake tofu. You add other spices as you cook.

Reprinted by permission of DFW Vegetarian: dfwnetmall.com/veg/

Glazed Tofu

Baked tofu can be glazed or marinated:

½ cup tamari soy sauce or Bragg's Liquid Aminos
1 tablespoon molasses
2 teaspoons peanut, sesame, olive, or canola oil

1 tablespoon lemon or lime juice
Salt and black pepper (unless used in baking)

1. Combine above ingredients.
2. Pour over 1 pound of baked tofu in a large skillet, over medium heat.
3. Move skillet around to coat tofu and keep it from sticking. Cook until sauce is syrupy and tofu is shiny with glaze. Stop cooking before it gets sticky.

Note: Commercial barbecue sauce, Thai peanut sauce, and hoisin sauce also glaze tofu nicely.

Reprinted by permission of DFW Vegetarian: dfwnetmall.com/veg/

Tofu Fajitas

Baked tofu (p. 144)

Onions
Peppers
Store-bought fajita seasonings

Mushrooms
Tortilla

1. Grill baked tofu with onions, peppers, fajita seasoning, and mushrooms.
2. Add salsa and avocado and wrap in a tortilla.

Reprinted by permission of DFW Vegetarian: dfwnetmall.com/veg/

Super Nachos

Layer:

Warmed refried beans
Salsa
Nacho Sauce (see p. 139)

Shredded lettuce
Chopped tomatoes

Serve with tortilla chips.

SOUPS AND CHILI

Pumpkin Soup

Serves 6

2 tablespoons olive oil
½ cup coarsely chopped onion
½ cup coarsely chopped celery
1 15-ounce can pumpkin (not pumpkin pie mix)
1 cup vegetable broth

1 cup fortified soymilk
1 15-ounce can black beans (optional)
1 cup frozen corn kernels (optional)
¼ cup (or more to taste) salsa
Vegan sour cream (Tofutti makes a tasty brand or see p. 140.)

1. In a large saucepan, sauté the onion and celery in the olive oil over medium heat until tender, about six minutes.
2. Add the pumpkin, vegetable broth, and soymilk and blend well.
3. Stir in the optional black beans and/or corn and heat thoroughly.
4. Stir in the salsa just before serving. Top each serving with a dollop of sour cream.

Corn Chowder

Serves 8

1 large onion, coarsely chopped
1 clove garlic, minced
1 green bell pepper, coarsely chopped
½ cup chopped celery
3 tablespoons olive oil
6 medium potatoes, diced

2 cups vegetable broth
2½ cups frozen corn kernels
2 cups fortified plain soymilk
½ teaspoon dried sage
½ teaspoon dried rosemary
½ teaspoon dried basil
Salt and pepper to taste

1. Sauté the onion, garlic, green pepper, and celery in the olive oil for two minutes.
2. Add the potatoes and vegetable broth.
3. Simmer over low heat until potatoes are tender.
4. Add the corn, soymilk, and herbs and simmer for an additional five minutes. Season with salt and pepper.

Cream of Cauliflower Soup

Serves 6

2 tablespoons olive oil
2 tablespoons flour
2 cups unchicken broth

2 cups plain soymilk
Florets from 1-pound head of
   cauliflower

1. Warm the olive oil in a heavy-bottomed 4-quart pot over medium heat. Add the flour and stir for about three minutes, until the flour smells toasty.
2. Whisk in the unchicken broth, bring to a slow simmer, and continue whisking until smooth.
3. Whisk in the soymilk and the cauliflower.
4. Cover the pot and simmer gently over low heat for about 25 minutes. The florets should fall apart when you crush them with the back of a spoon against the inside of the pot.
5. Puree the soup in a blender. Season to taste with salt and pepper. Serve immediately.

Chili non Carne

Serves 4 to 6

> *This is a quick and easy low-fat vegetarian chili. You could add a can of beans if desired.*

1–2 tablespoons vegetable oil
½ cup chopped onions
1–2 cloves of garlic, minced or pressed
1 tablespoon chili powder
1 teaspoon cumin powder
1 teaspoon paprika
12-ounce package Lightlife meatless fat-free Smart Ground or other veggie substitute

1 15-ounce can crushed tomatoes
¼ teaspoon cayenne pepper
1 tablespoon tamari or good-quality soy sauce
2 teaspoons brown sugar or Sucanat (optional)
½ cup water

1. Heat oil in skillet. Add onions and sauté until soft. Add garlic, chili powder, cumin, and paprika. Stir and cook a couple of minutes.
2. Add Smart Ground, crushed tomatoes, cayenne, and tamari. Add more water, if needed to thin. Simmer over medium heat about 10 or 15 minutes.

Copyright © Shirley Wilkes-Johnson

MAIN DISHES

Mushroom Stroganoff

Serves 4

1 onion, chopped
1 pound white button or baby bella mushrooms, sliced
3 Portobello mushroom caps, sliced
2 tablespoons olive oil
4 tablespoons vegetable broth powder or unchicken stock powder
¼ teaspoon freshly ground nutmeg

1½ teaspoons soy sauce
¼ teaspoon mustard powder
1 15-ounce can garbanzo beans (chickpeas)
2 teaspoons apple cider vinegar
10 ounces noodles or 1 cup brown rice
1 12-ounce box soft silken tofu

1. Warm the oil and, over medium heat, sauté the onions and mushrooms until they are soft (about 10 minutes).
2. Add the broth powder, seasonings, garbanzo beans (chickpeas), and vinegar. Cover and simmer over low heat for about 10 minutes.
3. Meanwhile, in a separate large pot, cook the noodles until al dente or boil the rice.
4. Empty the tofu into a blender and add some of the liquid from the mushroom mixture. Blend until the tofu is creamy. (But don't taste! The seasonings are with the mushrooms, and this will taste, as it is, rather bland.)
5. Add the creamed tofu to the mushroom mixture, and over very low heat, warm the mixture until heated through.
6. Serve over the cooked noodles or the rice.

Comforting Pot Pie

Serves 4 to 6

> *Plan ahead! Freeze a pound of tofu a couple of days in advance, then defrost it the night before. The following day, before you start cooking, let it drain in a strainer. It needs some moisture so don't squeeze out the liquid.*

Filling

1 pound defrosted firm tofu	1 cup chopped onions
1 tablespoon flour	1 cup chopped carrots
1 tablespoon nutritional yeast flakes	1 cup sliced mushrooms
1 tablespoon Bragg's Liquid Aminos	½ cup peas, fresh or frozen
2 tablespoons peanut oil	1 tablespoon minced fresh
1 medium-sized potato, diced	parsley leaves

1. Preheat the oven to 350° F and lightly oil a deep-dish pie plate or a 1½-quart casserole dish.

Make the filling

2. Cut the tofu into ¼-inch cubes. Mix the flour and nutritional yeast together. Add the tofu cubes and toss till coated.
3. Heat the peanut oil in a large skillet, add the tofu, sprinkle the Bragg's Liquid Aminos over the tofu, and brown the tofu.
4. When the tofu is golden and crisp, remove from the skillet into a large bowl.
5. Meanwhile, cook the potato in boiling, salted water until tender. Drain, and add to the tofu.
6. Heat 1 tablespoon olive oil in the skillet and add the onions and carrots. Cover the skillet and cook, stirring occasionally, until tender.
7. Add the onions and carrots to the tofu and potatoes.
8. Sauté the mushrooms. Add them, the peas, and the parsley to the mixing bowl.

Make the gravy

Gravy

2 cups vegetable stock
2½ tablespoons tamari soy sauce
½ teaspoon dried thyme
Salt

Freshly ground pepper
2 tablespoons cornstarch, dissolved
   in 3 tablespoons water
¼ cup soymilk or soy cream

1. Using the same skillet, add the stock, tamari, thyme, salt, and pepper and bring to a boil over medium-high heat.
2. Reduce the heat to medium-low, whisk the cornstarch and water together, and then add to the stock, whisking as you do.
3. Continue to whisk as the stock mixture boils for about one minute.
4. Turn off the heat, and whisk in the soymilk or soy cream.
5. Taste, adjust seasonings, and then add to the tofu mixture.

Make the crust

Crust

1¼ cup whole wheat pastry flour
¼ cup wheat germ
¼ teaspoon salt

⅛ cup olive oil, chilled
⅛ cup corn oil
2–4 tablespoons cold water

1. Combine the flour, wheat germ, and salt in a food processor. Pulse until they are blended together.
2. Add the oils and process until the mixture is crumbly. While the food processor is running, drizzle in the cold water 1 tablespoon at a time. Suddenly, the mixture will form a ball as it circles the food processor. Stop adding water the minute it does, and stop processing.
3. Lightly flour a work surface, and roll out the dough so that it is slightly larger than the casserole dish.
4. Gently place the crust over the casserole and its filling. Pinch the edges to seal. Cut four to six 1-inch slits in the top crust to allow steam to escape.
5. Bake at 350° F until heated and the crust is nicely browned, 40 to 45 minutes.

Variations: Easy Puff Pastry Crust

1 sheet Pepperidge Farm puff pastry

Follow the directions for defrosting the puff pastry. On a floured board, roll out the puff pastry sheet to slightly bigger than your casserole or pie dish. Cut the pastry to fit the top of the dish and place on top of the pot pie. Bake until the puff pastry has puffed up and is golden.

Squash Ribbon Sauté

Serves 2 to 3

> *Fresh vegetables seem especially interesting and flavorful when sliced in ribbons and blended with a fragrant and robust pesto.*

Pesto (Double this for generous servings of pesto.)

1 teaspoon olive oil (optional)
1 clove garlic, minced
¾ cup parsley, coarsely chopped
½ cup walnuts
½ teaspoon salt
4 teaspoons fresh lemon juice
Water to achieve desired consistency

Vegetables

1–2 medium zucchini, ends removed, thinly sliced lengthwise with a vegetable peeler
1–2 medium yellow crookneck squash, thinly sliced lengthwise
¾ cup cooked black beans
1 cup chopped fresh tomatoes
1 cup fresh corn kernels

Time-saving tip: Before you begin, measure and set out on your counter all of the ingredients for both pesto and vegetables.

1. In a blender or food processor combine all pesto ingredients and process until smooth. Stop the blender to push down the contents as necessary, and add water to achieve a thick, creamy consistency.
2. Place a little water in a large, nonstick skillet. Add squash ribbons, beans, tomatoes, corn, and 1 tablespoon of pesto. Cover and cook, stirring often, for four minutes. Uncover and continue cooking until squash is barely tender, about six minutes.
3. Transfer mixture to a large bowl, garnish with sprigs of parsley and generous dollops of pesto on top.

Copyright © Kay Bushnell

Linguine with Olives, Tomatoes, and Fresh Herbs

Serves 4

Use a mixture of olives (black, Kalamata, green, etc.) and enjoy the fresh taste of a Mediterranean garden in one delicious dish.

¾ cup mixed olives (black, Kalamata, etc.), pitted and sliced
1 tablespoon drained capers, chopped
1 medium garlic clove, pressed
¼ cup minced fresh parsley leaves
1 tablespoon minced fresh mint (or basil) leaves
2 medium tomatoes, diced

1 tablespoon minced fresh oregano
1 tablespoon extra-virgin olive oil
¼–½ cup chopped walnuts
Salt to taste
Pepper to taste
8–12 ounces linguine, cooked according to directions, and drained

1. Place olives, capers, garlic, herbs, and tomatos in a bowl large enough to hold the cooked pasta. Drizzle with olive oil and toss gently. Allow flavors to blend for at least 15 minutes.
2. Cook and drain pasta, then add to the bowl of herbs. Combine pasta and herbs gently and blend in the walnuts. Season with salt and pepper to taste. Serve at room temperature or slightly warmed.

Copyright © Kay Bushnell

Pad Thai

Serves 2 heartily

This was prepared by two young teens, Kate Wilkerson Sturla and Nora Boyd, for Animal Place's Veggie Cook-Off.

6 ounces rice noodles

Sauce

3 tablespoons fresh lemon or lime juice
3 tablespoons catsup
1 tablespoon sugar
¼ cup soy sauce

Stir-fry

1–2 tablespoons vegetable oil
4 garlic cloves, minced

1 fresh green jalapeno pepper, seeded and minced
2 carrots, grated (about 2 cups)
¼ pound mung bean sprouts (about 1½ cups)
4 scallions, finely chopped (about ¾ cup)
2 tablespoons peanuts, chopped (optional)
2 tablespoons cilantro, finely chopped (optional)

1. In a covered pan, bring the water to a rolling boil; stir in the rice noodles and cook for five to seven minutes. Drain the noodles, rinse them well under cool water, and set aside.
2. In a small bowl, combine the sauce ingredients; set aside.
3. Heat the oil in a medium skillet on medium-high heat. Add the garlic and jalapeno; stir for a moment. Stir in the grated carrots and fry for one to two minutes.
4. Add the sauce, noodles, bean sprouts, and scallions. Stir everything together. When the ingredients are warm, about one minute, remove to a platter.
5. Garnish with the peanuts and cilantro if you wish.

Copyright © Animal Place

Millet Croquettes

Serves approximately 4

> *Croquettes are patties that don't need buns or anything because they are so good on their own. Millet is perfect for them. You can flavor them any way you like, and you can also eat them like a veggie burger.*

¾ cup millet
2 cups water
Large pinch of salt
6 tablespoons fine bread crumbs
½ bunch scallions (5–6), minced

½ bunch parsley, minced
1½ tablespoon shoyu
Cornmeal for dredging
Canola or coconut oil for frying

1. Wash and drain millet, and dry roast over high heat in a medium pot for 5 to 10 minutes, stirring constantly.
2. Add water and salt, cover, and bring to a boil. Simmer 40 minutes or until water is absorbed.
3. Put millet in a large bowl with bread crumbs and let cool. Squeeze grain until sticky.
4. Add the scallions, parsley, and shoyu to millet.
5. Heat ½-inch of oil in a large skillet.
6. With wet hands, form croquettes. Make sure they are evenly flat, without bulges in the middle or sides that are thinner than the middle. Dredge in cornmeal.
7. When oil is rippling, add croquettes to skillet and fry until golden brown on each side. Flip, carefully, once during cooking.
8. Drain on paper towels.

Adapted by Lagusta Yearwood from a recipe by the Natural Gourmet Cookery School.

Sloppy "Janes"

Serves 4

2 tablespoons oil
1 pound frozen firm tofu, defrosted, with excess liquid squeezed out, or 1 pound Lightlife Gimme Lean! Ground Beef Style
2 cloves garlic, minced
1 medium onion, chopped
1 green pepper, diced
1 tablespoon chili powder
½ teaspoon cumin
½ teaspoon salt
⅛ teaspoon freshly ground black pepper
1 jar tomato sauce (Muir Glen tomato-basil sauce is a good brand for this, but pick your favorite.)
1 tablespoon Dijon mustard (optional)
3 tablespoons hoisin sauce
2 tablespoons tamari soy sauce

1. Heat 1 tablespoon oil in a large skillet. Add tofu or Gimme Lean and cook until browned over medium-high heat.
2. Transfer this to a bowl.
3. Heat skillet over medium-high heat with the remaining 1 tablespoon oil.
4. Add the garlic, green pepper, and onion, and cook until the onion is translucent (about five minutes).
5. Add chili powder, cumin, salt, and pepper. Cook for about two minutes.
6. Add tomato sauce, hoisin sauce, mustard, and tamari. Simmer for five minutes.
7. Add the cooked tofu or Gimme Lean. Simmer 10 minutes to blend flavors. Adjust the seasonings. Serve over burger buns.

Shish Kebobs

Yields 4 servings

Marinade for Shish Kabobs

2 crushed garlic cloves
⅓ cup tamari soy sauce
⅛ cup vegetable oil
5 tablespoons brown rice syrup
¼ cup apple cider vinegar
¼ cup apple juice
Minced fresh ginger root

Vegetables

Onions, mushrooms, red bell peppers, cherry tomatoes, pineapple pieces, and fresh figs if they are in season

Protein: Tofu or tempeh or seitan

1. Fix marinade and let sit while you prepare the vegetables. Thread the skewers with the vegetables, fruit, and your choice of protein. Place on tray.
2. Cover with marinade and let sit for 30 minutes, turning several times so that all sides are equally bathed in the marinade.
3. Grill.

Serve on rice or couscous with leftover marinade.

Tofu Tacos

Makes 4 tacos

Firm tofu makes a quick and delicious taco filling. You can also use frozen tofu in this recipe. Freezing tofu changes its texture significantly, making it very spongelike and chewy. To use frozen tofu, first thaw it, then squeeze out the excess water in it by squeezing it just as you would squeeze a sponge. Then crumble the tofu and proceed with the recipe.

1 tablespoon oil
½ onion, chopped, or 1 tablespoon onion powder

2 cloves garlic, crushed, or 1 teaspoon garlic powder
1 small bell pepper, diced (optional)

½ pound firm tofu, crumbled
(about 1 cup)
1 tablespoon chili powder
1 tablespoon nutritional yeast flakes
(optional)
¼ teaspoon each cumin and oregano
1 tablespoon soy sauce

¼ cup tomato sauce
Corn tortillas
Green onions, chopped
Lettuce, washed and torn
Tomatoes, diced
Avocado, diced
Salsa or taco sauce

1. Sauté onion, garlic, and bell pepper in oil for two to three minutes, then add tofu, chili powder, yeast, cumin, oregano, and soy sauce. Cook three minutes then add tomato sauce and simmer over low heat until mixture is fairly dry.
2. For an oil-free taco, heat the tortilla in a heavy, ungreased skillet, flipping it from side to side until it is soft and pliable. Place a small amount of the tofu mixture in the center, fold the tortilla in half, and remove from heat. Garnish with onions, lettuce, tomatoes, avocado, and salsa.
3. For a traditional taco, heat 1 tablespoon of oil in a skillet. Place a tortilla in the skillet and add a spoonful of the tofu mixture to it. When the tortilla is warm and pliable, use a spatula to fold it in half. Cook the first side until crisp, then flip it and cook the other side. Garnish as above.

Copyright © Jennifer Raymond

Easy Baked Beans

Serves 4

1 15-ounce can pinto beans, drained
½ cup coarsely chopped onion
2 tablespoons blackstrap molasses
1 teaspoon lite vegetarian
Worcestershire sauce

2 tablespoons apple cider vinegar
1 teaspoon Dijon mustard
2 tablespoons chili sauce
⅛ teaspoon garlic powder
½ cup tomato sauce

Preheat oven to 350° F. Combine all of the ingredients in a casserole dish. Cover and bake for one hour.

Pilaf with Carrots and Raisins

Serves 8

4 tablespoons maple syrup
3 cups vegetable broth
1 cup thinly sliced carrots
2 tablespoons raisins
1 tablespoon canola oil

1½ cups brown rice
½ teaspoon salt
¼ teaspoon ground cardamom
¼ teaspoon ground cinnamon
¼ teaspoon ground nutmeg

1. Combine the maple syrup and vegetable broth in a medium saucepan. Cook over low heat for two minutes.
2. In a large skillet, sauté the carrots and raisins in the oil for 10 minutes. Add the rice and stir to coat with the oil. Stir in syrup and broth and rest of ingredients.
3. Heat to a boil; reduce heat and simmer covered for about 40 minutes or until all of the liquid is absorbed.

Quinoa, Corn, and Potatoes

Serves 8

1 large onion, coarsely chopped
3 cloves garlic, minced
1 tablespoon olive oil
2 cups diced new potatoes
1½ cups vegetable broth

1 cup quinoa
1½ cups frozen corn kernels
½ teaspoon dried oregano
½ teaspoon dried tarragon
Salt and pepper to taste

1. Sauté the onion and garlic in the oil over medium heat for two minutes. Add the potatoes and sauté for another minute. Add the rest of the ingredients.
2. Bring to a boil, reduce heat, cover, and simmer for 20 minutes or until all of the broth has been absorbed.

Orzo Pilaf

Serves 4

2 cups water
1 cup orzo
4 tablespoons unchicken vegetable
   broth powder

4 tablespoons nutritional
   yeast flakes
1 teaspoon garlic-infused olive oil

1. Bring water to boil.
2. As water is coming to boil, shake orzo in a jar with the broth powder.
3. Add the orzo, and return to a boil.
4. Lower the heat, add the nutritional yeast, and cook, covered, until all water is absorbed, about 15 minutes.
5. Toss with olive oil.

Optional: Stir in some sautéed mushrooms after you remove the orzo from the heat.

Stuffed Manicotti

Yields 4 servings

1 recipe Tofu "Ricotta"
   (see pp. 137–38)
1 clove garlic
3 tablespoons fresh parsley
1 packed cup basil leaves

½ teaspoon ground nutmeg
1 jar tomato sauce
1 box of shells or manicotti,
   cooked according to directions
   on the box.

1. Combine all ingredients except the pasta and tomato sauce in a food processer and blend until smooth.
2. Stuff shells or manicotti, cover with tomato sauce, and bake for 30 minutes at 350° F.

Stuffed Acorn Squash

A great Thanksgiving dish

Makes 4 cups of stuffing. Serves 8 people as a main dish, and 16 as a side dish.

4 small acorn squashes (no more than 1 pound each)
Oil

For the stuffing:

2 tablespoons sesame oil (you can use olive oil if you don't have sesame oil)
1 cup onions, finely chopped
2 cups mushrooms, sliced
1 cup celery, finely chopped

4 cloves garlic, minced
2 teaspoons poultry seasoning
3 tablespoons tamari soy sauce
¼ teaspoon sea salt
3 cups whole wheat bread, cubed (be sure to select a bread that wasn't baked with eggs, milk, cheese, or whey)
½ cup fresh parsley, chopped
½ cup chopped dried apricots (for a real treat use glacé [sweetened] apricots)

1. Preheat the oven to 350° F.
2. Cut the squashes in half across the width of the squash. Scoop out the seeds. Lightly coat the edges of the squash with oil, place on a baking sheet cut side down, and bake for about 40 minutes. Remove from the oven. The squash should be tender when pierced by a fork or knife.
3. Meanwhile, prepare the stuffing. Heat the oil in a large nonstick frying pan over medium heat. Add onions, mushrooms, celery, and garlic. Stir. Sprinkle poultry seasoning over vegetables. Dissolve the salt in the tamari soy sauce and add to the pan. Stir, then cover, and continue to cook until the vegetables are done, about five minutes. Remove from heat.
4. Add the cubed bread, parsley, and apricots. Mix well. Then cover and set aside for several minutes. The bread should absorb the moisture from the vegetables. The stuffing should be well seasoned and moist, but not wet.
5. The recipe can be prepared to this point ahead of time.
6. Just before serving, stuff each squash with about ½ cup of stuffing. Bake in a 375°F oven for about 15 to 20 minutes, until thoroughly heated.

VEGGIES AND SALADS

Roasted Red Pepper

Great for adding to salads and pasta dishes, especially lasagna.

Red pepper   Olive oil

1. Preheat oven to 450° F.
2. Cut a red pepper in half, and remove the seeds and the ribs of the pepper. Lightly coat the pepper halves inside and out with olive oil. Place with the skin side up on a pan.
3. Bake until the pepper skin has blistered and appears darkened, almost black, and has begun to puff away from the body of the pepper— about 30 minutes. Remove from the oven and let cool for a few minutes. The charred skin should be easy to peel loose. Slice the skinned pepper, and place in a little olive oil while it cools.

❧

Lentil Salad

Serves 4 to 6

This is a great summer salad.

Salad

1½ cups lentils, rinsed and picked over
1 cup chopped onions
2 garlic cloves, chopped
4 cups water
1 cup finely chopped red or green bell peppers
1 cup finely chopped celery
1 cup finely chopped red onions

Curried Mango Tofu Dressing

1 12-ounce box of soft silken tofu
1 tablespoon fresh lime juice
4 tablespoons prepared mango chutney
2 teaspoons curry powder
2 teaspoons finely minced red onions

1. Combine the lentils, onions, garlic, and water in a large saucepan.
2. Bring the ingredients to a boil, reduce the heat, and simmer for 30 to 40 minutes. The lentils should be tender, but don't cook them too long because they will become mushy.

3. Using a nonmetal bowl, combine the peppers, celery, and red onions.
4. When the lentils are tender, drain them, and, while still warm, place them in the bowl. Stir them together with the raw vegetables. Set the bowl aside for 15 minutes.
5. In a blender, process the tofu and lime juice. Empty into a bowl, stir in the chutney, curry powder, and red onion.
6. Stir the dressing into the lentil-vegetable mixture. Serve.

Greek Salad

Serves 4 to 6

1 crisp head lettuce or 2 cups mixed
   greens—including romaine hearts
   and watercress
Olive oil
Lemon juice or vinegar
Salt and pepper
1 pound Tofu "Feta Cheese"
   (see p. 137)
1 medium cucumber, sliced but
   not peeled

2½ cups whole cherry tomatoes
½ pound Greek olives, green
   and black
1 small green bell pepper, sliced
Avocado, sliced
Onion, sliced
⅓ cup parsley, coarsely chopped

1. Line a large oblong or oval platter with the outer leaves of the lettuce.
2. Tear the remaining lettuce leaves into small pieces into a bowl. Toss them with a little olive oil, lemon juice or vinegar, and some salt and pepper. Arrange the lettuce in a mound on the platter.
3. Sprinkle the sliced cucumber with salt and pepper. Arrange the cucumbers in an overlapping pattern near the edge of the platter.
4. Within the ring of cucumber slices, arrange a ring of tofu feta.
5. Within the ring of tofu feta, place the green olives.
6. In the center, place the cherry tomatoes and the black olives.
7. Place the sliced peppers, avocado, and onions so as to decorate the salad with these slices.
8. Sprinkle the entire salad with olive oil and lemon juice, and the oregano. Serve.

Autumn Wheat Berry Salad

Serves 6 to 8

This salad is also great as a sandwich filling. Split pita bread, line with lettuce leaves, add a scoop of the salad, and top with a few toasted pumpkin seeds.

2 cups wheat berries
1½ cup celery, diced
Water
1 cup green onions, sliced
1 cup cooked black beans
1 cup cooked kidney beans
½ cup red onion, diced
1 15-ounce can diced tomatoes, drained
⅓ cup freshly chopped parsley

Dressing

⅓ cup olive oil
¼ cup red wine vinegar
2 tablespoons tamari soy sauce
1½ tablespoons dried oregano
1 tablespoon chili powder
1 tablespoon garlic, minced
1 tablespoon fresh ginger, minced
1 teaspoon salt
¼ teaspoon pepper
Toasted pumpkin seeds for garnish

Cover wheat berries with water and leave them to soak for several hours or overnight.

1. Drain, place in a pot, and cover with fresh water. Cook wheat berries over medium-high heat for two to three hours or until they are tender. Drain well and transfer to a bowl.
2. Toss cooked wheat berries with celery, green onions, both types of beans, red onion, tomatoes, and parsley.
3. In a small bowl, whisk together dressing ingredients. Pour dressing over the wheat berry mixture and toss gently to mix. Garnish individual servings with toasted pumpkin seeds.

Copyright © Beverly Lynn Bennett

Ensalada de Frijoles

Serves 2 to 4

> *This salad is a complete one-dish meal. Prepare one plate for each person being served.*

2 cups cooked brown rice
6 cups prewashed salad mix
1 carrot grated or cut in thin strips
1 15-ounce can of black beans, drained
1 cup diced jicama
1 tomato, diced or cut into wedges
1 15-ounce can corn, drained

¼–½ cup cilantro leaves (optional)
½ avocado, thinly sliced (optional)
¼ cup salsa (you choose the heat!)
¼ cup seasoned rice vinegar
1 garlic clove, crushed or pressed
Additional salsa for topping

Divide the brown rice among the plates. Top with salad and a sprinkling of carrots. Rinse the beans, then sprinkle them over each of the salads. Add the jicama, tomato, corn, cilantro, and avocado. Mix the salsa, seasoned rice vinegar, and crushed garlic. Sprinkle over each of the salads, then top with a generous spoonful of salsa.

Copyright © Jennifer Raymond

Broccoli and "Bacon" Salad

Serves 6

8 ounces Fakin' Bakin bacon substitute
1 pound fresh broccoli

¼ cup raisins
¼ cup Vegenaise eggless mayonnaise
Salt and pepper to taste

1. Cook Fakin' Bakin according to package directions and crumble or cut into small pieces.
2. Cut the broccoli into small florets.
3. In a large pot, bring a quart of water to a boil.
4. Drop the broccoli into the water and boil for one minute, just to blanch it.

5. Drain and rinse the broccoli with cold water.
6. Toss with Fakin' Bakin, raisins, and mayonnaise and season to taste with salt and pepper.

Crunchy Onion Rings

Serves 4

Shirley Wilkes-Johnson writes, "I based this recipe on one I found in a February 1999 issue of Shape *magazine. But their recipe called for buttermilk and egg whites. I think anyone would like my version better. You've got to try these. They are easy to make and are almost fat free! These would go great with a veggie burger! You can also use bell pepper rings."*

2 large onions, sliced into ½-inch rings	2 teaspoons paprika
2 cups soymilk	1 teaspoon salt
2 tablespoons lemon juice or apple cider vinegar	1 cup yellow salad mustard
	1 cup water
2 cups unbleached white flour	3 cups corn flake crumbs *

1. In a large bowl, mix soymilk and lemon juice or vinegar. Toss in sliced onions and coat them with the mixture. Set aside.
2. Preheat oven to 350° F and spray a baking sheet with nonstick spray.
3. In a shallow bowl, mix flour, paprika, and salt.
4. In another shallow bowl, mix mustard and water until it is the consistency of a beaten egg.
5. Place the corn flakes in a third shallow bowl.
6. Take each soymilk-coated onion ring and dredge it in the flour, then dip it into the mustard batter and finally into the corn flakes, coating the onion rings in each process.
7. Place the onion rings on a sprayed baking sheet and spray the onions lightly with the nonstick spray.
8. Bake about 15 minutes or until golden brown.

* You can buy corn flake crumbs or make your own with Kellogg's Corn Flakes cereal. Put corn flakes into a food processor and process until fine but not powdery.

Copyright © Shirley Wilkes-Johnson

Crunchy Green Beans

Serves 4

1 pound fresh green beans
2 teaspoons olive oil
¼ cup slivered toasted almonds

¼ cup sliced water chestnuts
Salt and pepper to taste

Steam the green beans until just tender. Toss them with the olive oil, almonds, water chestnuts, and season with salt and pepper.

Kale with Cinnamon

Serves 4

1 medium onion, minced
1 tablespoon olive oil
1 clove garlic, minced
⅛ teaspoon ground cinnamon

1 pound fresh kale, finely chopped
1 cup vegetable broth
1 teaspoon red wine vinegar
Salt and pepper to taste

1. Sauté the onion in oil for four minutes. Add the garlic and cook for an additional two minutes.
2. Stir in the cinnamon and add the kale, tossing to coat with the onion and cinnamon mixture.
3. Add the vegetable broth. Cover and simmer for 15 minutes. Season with vinegar, salt, and pepper.

Scalloped Potatoes

Serves 4 to 6

4 cups potatoes, peeled and
   thinly sliced
2 medium onions, chopped
⅓ cup flour

Salt and pepper
⅓ cup margarine
2 quarts soymilk or combination of
   soymilk and unchicken stock

1. Preheat oven to 350° F.
2. Oil a 9 × 13-inch pan.
3. Put a layer of sliced potatoes on the bottom, add onions, sprinkle some flour over the vegetables, and a little salt and pepper. Dot with a little of the margarine.
4. Repeat, making several layers. Omit flour when you reach the top layer.
5. Pour soymilk or soymilk/unchicken stock combination slowly over the vegetables until the top layer is almost covered. Bake for one and a half to two hours, until the potatoes are soft when tested with a fork and the soymilk is thickened.

Creamed Greens

Serves 6

1½ pounds fresh greens (collards,
   kale, turnip, or mustard greens)
2 tablespoons white flour

2 tablespoons olive oil
1 cup fortified plain soymilk
Salt and pepper to taste

1. Tear the greens into small pieces and place in a large pot of boiling water.
2. Reduce heat and simmer for 15 minutes.
3. In a separate pot, stir the flour into the oil. Stir over low heat for four minutes. Slowly stir in the soymilk. Raise heat to a boil, then reduce to simmer, stirring until thickened.
4. Drain the greens and stir into the cream sauce. Season with salt and pepper.

DESSERTS

Chocolate-chip Cake

Makes 10 slices

1½ cups white flour
1 cup sugar
1 teaspoon baking soda
⅛ teaspoon salt
¼ cup canola or soy oil

1 teaspoon vanilla extract
1 tablespoon apple cider vinegar
1 cup cold water
1 cup semisweet chocolate chips

1. Preheat oven to 350° F.
2. In a large mixing bowl, stir together the flour, sugar, baking soda, and salt.
3. In a separate bowl, stir together the oil, vanilla, vinegar, and water. Pour the liquid over the flour mixture. Stir well to combine.
4. Pour batter into an ungreased 8 × 8-inch pan. Sprinkle the chocolate chips over the top. Bake for 35 minutes, until the cake pulls away from the side of the pan and a cake tester inserted in the center of the cake comes out clean (except for melted chocolate!).

Mile-high Carob or Chocolate Layer Cake

12 to 14 servings, one three-layer cake

Really Fudgey Frosting

⅓ cup water
¼ cup cornstarch
¾ cup maple syrup
½ cup smooth almond butter
⅓ cup unsweetened, roasted carob
    powder or unsweetened cocoa
    powder
2 teaspoons vanilla extract
Approximately ¼ cup low-fat, non-
    dairy milk, more or less as needed

Wet Ingredients

1¾ cup unbleached cane sugar
1 12-ounce package lite silken tofu
    (firm) crumbled

1 cup water
⅓ cup canola oil
2 teaspoons apple cider vinegar
1 teaspoon vanilla extract

Dry Ingredients

2 cups whole wheat pastry flour
½ cup sweetened, roasted carob
    powder or unsweetened cocoa
    powder, sifted
1 tablespoon non-aluminum baking
    powder (such as Rumford)
¼ teaspoon salt

1. To make the frosting, place the water and cornstarch in a 1-quart saucepan, and stir until the cornstarch is dissolved. Stir in the maple syrup. Place the saucepan over medium-high heat and bring the mixture to a boil, stirring constantly. After the mixture is very thick and smooth, reduce the heat to medium-low, and continue to cook, stirring constantly, for one minute. Scrape the mixture into a food processor fitted with a metal blade. Add the remaining frosting ingredients, and process until very smooth. Use the smallest amount of milk necessary to process the mixture and make a very thick but spreadable frosting. If more milk is required, add 1 to 2 teaspoons at a time until the desired consistency is achieved. Set aside.
2. Preheat the oven to 350° F. Mist three 9-inch round cake pans with nonstick cooking spray, and set them aside.
3. Place the wet ingredients in a blender, and process until smooth.
4. Place the dry ingredients in a large mixing bowl, and stir them together. Pour the wet ingredients into the dry ingredients, and beat well using a wire whisk or electric beater to make a smooth batter.

5. Pour the batter equally into the prepared baking pans. Shake the pans back and forth to even out the batter, then tap the pans on a countertop to rid the batter of any air pockets. Bake until a cake tester inserted in the center of each cake comes out clean, about 25 to 30 minutes.

6. Remove the pans from the oven, and place them on cooling racks. Allow the cakes to cool for 10 to 15 minutes. Then turn them out of the pans, and allow them to cool completely.

7. To frost the cake, place one of the layers on an attractive serving plate, flat side up. Spread the top of the layer carefully with one-quarter of the frosting. Place the second cake layer, flat side up, on top of the first, and flatten gently with your hand. Spread the top of the second layer with one-third of the remaining frosting. Place the third layer, flat side up, on top and again flatten gently. Frost the top and sides of the cakes using all of the remaining frosting. Using a flat-edged knife or icing spatula, make quick movements to create swirls on the top and sides of the cake. Let stand for about one hour to set the frosting. Serve at room temperature. Store leftover cake covered, in the refrigerator.

Copyright © Joanne Stepaniak

❧

Garden-Kissed Snack Cake

¾ cup pitted dates
½ cup water
½ cup frozen orange juice concentrate
¾ cup apple juice
⅓ cup orange juice
Zest of 1 orange
2 tablespoons canola oil

1 teaspoon vanilla
2 cups whole wheat pastry flour
1 tablespoon cornstarch
2 teaspoons baking powder
2 teaspoons baking soda
⅔ cup shredded carrots
⅔ cup shredded zucchini
⅓ cup chopped walnuts

1. Preheat oven to 350° F.
2. In a small saucepan, cook dates in ½ cup water, uncovered, over medium heat for seven minutes. In a food processor or blender, puree dates with any remaining water left in the pan and the orange juice concentrate.

3. Add both fruit juices, orange zest, oil, and vanilla, and blend for 30 seconds.
4. In a bowl, sift together flour, cornstarch, baking powder, and baking soda. Add pureed mixture to the dry ingredients and stir until batter is smooth. Fold in carrots and zucchini.
5. Pour batter into a greased 9-inch pan and sprinkle walnuts over the top. Bake for 25 to 30 minutes or until a toothpick comes out clean. Allow to cool before removing from the pan.

Copyright © Beverly Lynn Bennett

Banana Cake

Jennifer Raymond writes: "This cake really doesn't need frosting, though it can be frosted with the Tofu Cream Frosting if desired."

2 cups flour (unbleached or whole wheat pastry)
1½ teaspoons baking soda
½ teaspoon salt
1 cup raw sugar or other sweetener
⅓ cup oil

4 ripe bananas, mashed (about 2½ cups)
¼ cup water
1 teaspoon vanilla
1 cup chopped walnuts (optional)

1. Preheat oven to 350° F.
2. Mix flour, baking soda, and salt together in a large mixing bowl.
3. In another bowl, beat sugar and oil together, then stir in the mashed bananas, water, and vanilla and mix thoroughly.
4. Mix with dry ingredients, and stir in walnuts if desired.
5. Spread into a greased 9-inch square pan, and bake from 45 to 50 minutes, until a toothpick inserted into the center comes out clean.

Copyright © Jennifer Raymond

Tofu Cream Frosting

It is important that the tofu, which is the basis of this frosting, be fresh. Fresh tofu has a neutral or slightly sweet taste.

1 cup firm tofu
2 tablespoons oil
2 tablespoons fresh lemon juice

3 to 4 tablespoons rice syrup
¼ teaspoon salt
½ teaspoon vanilla

Combine ingredients in a blender and blend until very smooth. Scrape sides of blender often with a rubber spatula to get frosting completely smooth.

Makes enough to generously frost one 9 × 9-inch cake.

Copyright © Jennifer Raymond

Peanut Butter Cookies

Makes 2 dozen cookies

¼ cup soft margarine
½ cup firmly packed brown sugar
½ cup sugar
⅔ cup smooth peanut butter
¼ cup water

½ teaspoon vanilla extract
1 to 1½ cups white flour
½ teaspoon baking soda
½ teaspoon salt

1. Preheat oven to 375° F.
2. Cream together the margarine, sugars, and peanut butter. Add the water and vanilla and mix thoroughly.
3. In a separate bowl, sift together the flour, baking soda, and salt. Add this dry mixture, ¼ cup at a time, to the peanut butter mixture. The dough will be very stiff.
4. Form into balls about the size of walnuts and place on an ungreased cookie sheet. Using a fork dipped into water, flatten each cookie twice, turning the fork to make a crisscross design.
5. Bake for 10 to 12 minutes until lightly browned.

Maple Almond Pudding

Serves 4

2 tablespoons cornstarch
2 tablespoons unsweetened apple
  juice or water
2 cups soymilk
¼ teaspoon salt

6 tablespoons maple syrup
2 tablespoons unsalted almond
  butter
1 tablespoon vanilla extract

1. Combine cornstarch and apple juice or water. Stir so that the cornstarch dissolves.
2. Pour soymilk into a double boiler, and gently heat over boiling water.
3. Whisk in the salt, maple syrup, and the almond butter.
4. Add the cornstarch and water, and continue whisking until the mixture is thick.
5. Whisk in the vanilla.
6. Distribute into four pudding cups, cool, chill, and serve.

Ginger Peachy Bread Pudding

Serves 9

1 28-ounce can sliced peaches
1 tablespoon cornstarch
6 cups cubed whole grain bread
  (about 8 slices)
1¾ cups soymilk or rice milk
⅓ cup packed brown sugar
¾ cup golden raisins
½ teaspoon ginger

½ teaspoon cinnamon
¼ teaspoon ground nutmeg
¼ teaspoon salt
1 teaspoon vanilla
¼ cup finely chopped crystallized
  ginger (optional)
2 tablespoons brown sugar

1. Drain the liquid from the peaches into a large mixing bowl and mix it with the cornstarch.
2. Stir to dissolve any lumps, then add the bread cubes, soy or rice milk, brown sugar, raisins, ginger, cinnamon, nutmeg, salt, and vanilla.
3. Mix well.

4. Stir in the crystallized ginger if desired.
5. Chop the peaches and stir them into the mixture.
6. Spread in a 9 × 9-inch baking dish, then sprinkle the top with brown sugar and let stand five minutes while the oven preheats to 350° F.
7. Bake for 35 minutes. Serve warm or cooled.

Copyright © Jennifer Raymond

❧

Cheeseque Cake from Buffalo

Made by some young women who came to hear me speak in Buffalo in 2001. They wrote out the recipe for this delicious and easy "cheeseque" cake, as they called it, but I never got their names.

Crust

1 package Midel cookie-of-choice
4 tablespoons margarine

Filling

3 8-ounce packages of Tofutti cream cheese

¾ cup maple syrup
1 teaspoon vanilla
½ teaspoon almond extract
2 tablespoons lemon juice (optional)
5 teaspoons arrowroot powder
6 ounces chocolate chips

1. Preheat oven to 350° F.
2. Crumble cookies, add the margarine, and press into a pie plate or springform pan.
3. In food processor or by hand, combine all ingredients except chocolate chips.
4. Spread three-quarters of the mixture over the cookie crust.
5. In a double boiler, melt the chocolate chips. Combine with the remainder of the filling mixture.
6. Swirl the chocolate mixture into the rest of the filling, being careful not to disturb the crust.
7. Bake for 45 minutes to one hour.
8. Let cool. And enjoy.

Pumpkin Cream Pie

Makes 1 pie

This recipe is easy and scrumptious. You might need more than one! One container of Tofutti Better than Cream Cheese will make two pies.

1 Keebler Graham Cracker
   Ready Crust
1 box silken tofu
1 15-ounce can solid pack pumpkin
½ cup Tofutti Better than Cream
   Cheese
½ cup Sucanat or turbinado sugar

¼ cup maple syrup
2 teaspoons vanilla extract
1 teaspoon cinnamon
½ teaspoon ground nutmeg
½ teaspoon ground ginger
¼ teaspoon cloves
¼ teaspoon allspice

1. Preheat oven to 350° F.
2. Puree tofu in a food processor until it is smooth. Scrape tofu off the sides of the processor and blend again.
3. Add pumpkin and blend. Again, scrape the sides and blend again.
4. Add Better than Cream Cheese, sugar, maple syrup, vanilla, and spices and blend well. The mixture should be smooth and creamy.
5. Pour the mixture into the prepared crust. Bake 50 minutes.
6. Turn off the oven. Without opening the door, leave pie to sit for another 50 minutes. Remove from the oven and let cool.
7. Cover and refrigerate overnight.

Appendix: An A–Z Guide to Vegetarian Foods

Brown rice syrup is a liquid sweetener derived from brown rice. It is a delicious alternative to honey and it works effectively in baked goods. (*See also* Fruit-source.) It is less sweet than honey, but if you use it as a honey substitute you might find that you do not have to increase the amount of brown rice syrup because the depth of its flavor adequately compensates for the cloying sweetness of honey. When using liquid sweeteners such as brown rice syrup, measure your oil first and then the measuring cup will have a coating that will allow the syrup to slide out.

"Chicken-flavored" vegetarian stock powder is available at many natural food stores. It can be used to make "unchicken" noodle soups, as an alternative flavoring for soup recipes that call for chicken stock. I also sprinkle some in a little water and cook broccoli in it until the water has evaporated or add a teaspoon or so to cream sauces.

Coffee substitutes are usually made from a combination of roasted barley, malt, chicory, rye, and beet root. Other ingredients may be figs, carob, almonds, and dates. They contain no caffeine. In baked goods they can be used with carob to provide an alternative to chocolate. The coffee substitute deepens the flavor and is suggestive of mocha. Many vegans enjoy coffee products; some health-conscious vegans opt for coffee substitutes. I have used Instant/Sipp Natural Coffee Substitute, but I have also encountered exotic offerings such as Teeccino Almond Amaretto Caffeine-Free Herbal Coffee.

Ener-G Egg Replacer is the brand name of a powder that one can use in the place of eggs. Its ingredients include potato starch, tapioca flour, dairy-free calcium lactate, calcium carbonate, citric acid, and carbohydrate gum. Mixing 1½ teaspoons egg replacer with two tablespoons water creates the equivalent of one egg. One can also use bananas, soft tofu, arrowroot powder, or cornstarch as a binder in baked goods.

Fruitsource is a liquid sweetener and fat replacer made from organic brown rice syrup and grape juice concentrate. It has the consistency of honey, an appealing amber color, and a wonderful aroma to it. Because of the grape juice, its sweetness is stronger than that of brown rice syrup.

Imagine Natural Garden Vegetable Soups are a line of soups from Imagine Foods. Their "no-chicken broth" is a convenient base for many soups.

Kombu is a stiff black sea vegetable, sold in almost footlong strips. It provides an instant stock when boiled for several minutes.

Mirin is a sweet Japanese cooking wine made from sweet rice. The best-quality mirin is made from sweet rice, rice *koji*, and water with no added sugar, alcohol, or fermenting agents.

Miso is a fermented soybean paste that adds flavor to sauces and soups. Some misos are made solely from soybeans and salt. Others are made from soybeans, salt, and a grain such as rice or barley, or legumes such as chickpeas. It is a fine source of high-quality protein. It provides a salty flavor and can mimic, at times, Parmesan cheese in some recipes. Avoid boiling miso once you have added it to a dish because intense heat will destroy its healthful enzymes. Keep refrigerated. Found in health food stores, natural food stores, and Asian food stores.

Nutritional yeast flakes refers to Red Star formula (T6635+) nutritional yeast flakes. Do not confuse it with brewer's yeast. Red Star nutritional yeast is an inactive yeast; it does not produce fermenting effects on baked goods. Instead, it is a rich source of B-complex vitamins, specifically riboflavin, niacin, thiamin, and biotin. It also provides protein when added to foods. If your local health food store does not carry it, it can be ordered from The Mail Order Catalog, PO Box 180, Summertown, TN 38483, 1-800-695-2241. Joanne Stepaniak's *The Nutritional Yeast Cookbook* and *The Uncheese Cookbook* provide numerous scrumptious recipes incorporating nutritional yeast flakes.

Puff pastry. Pepperidge Farm makes a frozen vegan puff pastry. Follow the instructions for defrosting the puff pastry, and use according to the recipe.

Shoyu. Like tamari, shoyu is naturally brewed soy sauce. It differs from tamari in that wheat, as well as soybean, salt, and water, has been used in the natural fermentation process.

Spectrum Spread is a nonhydrogenated vegetable shortening that is used instead of butter. I always keep some on hand for making scones and cobblers. Available in natural food stores.

Sucanat is a sugarcane sweetener. It contains more minerals, trace elements, and vitamins than table sugar. You can substitute it for refined sugar, one cup for one cup.

Tamari soy sauce is a naturally fermented soy sauce made from soybeans, salt, water and a starter called *koji*. It is nothing like commercial soy sauce, which is indebted to caramel for its dark brown color and to corn syrup for its sweetness. Tamari soy sauce's fermentation occurs through the introduction of a soybean starter.

Tofu is an inexpensive, versatile, high-quality protein, cholesterol-free, rich-in-calcium soybean product. It is made by a process similar to making cheese: soymilk is coagulated, drained, and then the curds are pressed into a cake. (Home tofu kits are now available.) The fear of tofu is due, in part, to its blandness. In fact, its "blandness" is what makes it so versatile because of its ability to absorb a variety of flavors. Tofu is labeled according to its water content. The less water it contains, the firmer the tofu is and the more likely it is to hold its shape in cooking. Regular tofu is packed in water, and usually found in plastic tubs in the refrigerator section of a health foods store, as well as the produce section of supermarkets. Keep it refrigerated. Silken tofu is creamy, smooth, and available in aseptic boxes that do not require refrigeration. If you are frying or baking tofu, use regular tofu. If you are using tofu in baked goods, creamy soups, puddings, or cream pies, use silken tofu.

Tofutti products are a line of products that contain no dairy, no cholesterol, no lactose, and no butterfat yet are amazingly similar to their dairy equivalents. Among the offerings from Tofutti are "Better than Sour Cream Sour Supreme" and "Better than Cream Cheese." They are remarkable substitutes for almost any recipe that calls for sour cream or cream cheese. For many years, one of my sons took for his school lunch a bagel with Better than Cream Cheese spread on it. A tablespoon of Sour Supreme is great added to some soups or on tortillas.

TVP is texturized vegetable protein. It is made from soy flour. After the soybean oil has been extracted, cooked under pressure, extruded, and dried the result is a dense textured food that is chewy and "meatlike." It is sold in granules, flakes, chunks, or slices. When rehydrated the granules resemble ground beef and the chunks have the texture and appearance of chunks of meat. Especially when cooked in certain ways, it is often mistaken for meat and it can be substituted for meat, such as hamburger, in recipes like "sloppy joes." TVP is an excellent source of protein and fiber and has zero cholesterol. The initials are the registered trademark of the Archer Daniels Midland Company.

Vegan margarine. Many margarines have some dairy products in them. Vegan margarines do not. An example is Earth Balance Natural Buttery Spread. Some brands, such as this one, are not hydrogenated and have no trans fatty acids. Spectrum Spread is also nonhydrogenated. It makes baked goods like cobblers and scones very delicious.

Vegetarian Worcestershire sauce may be carried by your local natural foods store, or you can order it from PANGEA (1-800-340-1200), 2381 Lewis Avenue, Rockville, MD 20852, or order online at www.veganstore.com.

Wheat Meat or Chicken Style Wheat Meat is one of the brands of seitan now available. Seitan is made from wheat gluten and is a good protein alternative for those who have soy allergies. Like tofu, it is versatile in its uses. Seitan is a high-protein, zero-cholesterol, low-fat meat alternative because of its chewy texture. In many recipes, you can veganize chicken recipes by substituting wheat meat or seitan for the amount of chicken called for in the recipe.

Acknowledgments

Thanks to Patti Breitman, friend, agent, change-agent, for suggesting this book. You believe in your writers, in vegans, and in all people—that we each in our own way can reach out and be present to others in need. Thanks to Pat Davis, friend, teacher, counselor, for suggesting that vegetarian teens needed support. You believe in young people and teach us adults how to trust them and allow for their growth; in this, you have helped me grow as a parent. Thanks to Evander Lomke, supportive and encouraging editor, for agreeing that a book like this was needed. All the youthful vegetarians and vegans who have invited me to their campuses, who have shared their experiences with me over lunch or dinner or through e-mail—thank you for allowing me a glimpse of your experiences, for your honesty, for your optimism, and for your good food! For parents who have told me of their joys and frustrations, thank you for supporting this project and reaching out through this book to other parents of vegetarian children. For the vegan chefs, who have shared recipes with me through the years, who continue to surprise me with their wonderfully creative minds: you witness to the abundance that is possible in life. I especially thank Beverly Lynn Bennett, Kay Bushnell, Karen Davis, Terry Jensen, Jennifer Raymond, Joanne Stepaniak, Kim Sturla, Shirley Wilkes-Johnson, and Lagusta Yearwood. I am grateful for the work of Ginny Messina, for helping to expand our understanding of vegetarian nutrition, for lending her expertise to this book, for writing a warm and welcoming chapter, and for supporting my work. Chapter 3, "Nutritional Issues for Vegetarians," is Copyright © Virginia Messina. Recipes as noted are Copyright the individual recipe creators. My parents, Lee Towne Adams and Muriel Adams, supported me as I found my footing as a vegetarian, and in all that I have tried to be as an activist and a writer. My children, Douglas and Benjamin, have helped me think about parenting and the inevitable mistakes we parents make. I am glad we can laugh about them and learn from them. Bruce, my partner, has taught me so much about parenting as we move through these experiences together, creating a supportive environment for me to travel and to write.

Metric-conversion Table

OVEN TEMPERATURE CHART

temperature	Fahrenheit (F)	Centigrade (C)	Gas Mark
	200	100	0
Very cool	225	110	1/4
	250	120	1/2
	275	140	1
Cool	300	150	2
Warm	325	170	3
Moderate	350	180	4
Moderately hot	375	190	5
Fairly hot	400	200	6
	425	220	7
Hot	450	230	8
	475	245	9
Very Hot	500	260	10

U.S. TO METRIC EQUIVALENTS

Volume

¼ teaspoon = 1.25 ml

½ teaspoon - 2.5 ml

¾ teaspoon = 3.75 ml

1 teaspoon = 5 ml

1 tablespoon = 15 ml

1 fluid oz. = 30 ml

¼ cup = 60 ml

⅓ cup = 79 ml

½ cup = 120 ml

⅓ cup = 158 ml

¼ cup = 180 ml

1 cup = 240 ml

2 cups (1 pint) = 480 ml

4 cups (1 quart) = .95 liter

4 quarts (1 gal.) = 3.8 liters

Weight

1 ounce = 28.4 grams

4 ounces (¼ pound) = 125 grams

8 ounces (½ pound) = 227.5 grams

12 ounces (¾ pound) = 375 grams

16 ounces (1 pound) = 455 grams